ICONS

Design for the
21st Century

Cover:
Ross Lovegrove, **Go magnesium** chair for Bernhardt USA, 2001
© Studio X, London (photo: John Ross)

Right page:
Shin + Tomoko Azumi, **Wireframe** chair and stool
(self-production), 1998

To stay informed about upcoming TASCHEN titles, please
request our magazine at www.taschen.com or write to
TASCHEN, Hohenzollernring 53, D–50672 Cologne,
Germany, Fax: +49-221-254919. We will be happy
to send you a free copy of our magazine which is filled
with information about all of our books.

Editorial coordination: Julia Krumhauer, Cologne
Design: UNA (London) designers
Production: Martina Ciborowius, Cologne

Printed in Italy
ISBN 3–8228–2779–7

Design for the
21st Century

Edited by Charlotte and Peter Fiell

TASCHEN

KÖLN LONDON LOS ANGELES MADRID PARIS TOKYO

With the unrelenting globalization of the free-market economy, so design has become a truly global phenomenon. Throughout the industrialized world, manufacturers of all types are increasingly recognizing and implementing design as an essential means of reaching new international audiences and of gaining competitive advantage. More than ever before, the products of design are shaping a world-wide material culture and impacting on the quality of our environment and daily lives. The importance of design, therefore, cannot be understated. For not only has design come to encompass an extraordinary range of functions, techniques, attitudes, ideas and values, all of them influencing our experience and perception of the world around us, but the choices we make today about the future direction of design will have a significant and possibly enduring effect on the quality of our lives and the environment in the years to come.

This book is first and foremost about the future of design. It focuses on those individuals who generally have the greatest input in the conception and planning of new products – designers. These are the creative thinkers able to identify and respond to the real needs and concerns of society, and whose decision-making can have a critical influence upon the nature and success of new products, manufacturing strategies and trends in the marketplace. What they think about the future really matters – thus *Design for the 21st Century* features the future vision statements and latest, most progressive work of 45 contemporary designers and design groups, drawn from a wide range of disciplines – product design, transportation, furniture, ceramics and glassware – and many different parts of the world, from

Europe to America, Finland, Brazil and Japan. Well-known figures such as Philippe Starck, Ron Arad, Ross Lovegrove and Marc Newson are joined by other, less familiar names who represent the equally important up-and-coming generation of designers. Also included are in-house designers who work for large corporations such as Apple Computer and Ford, and who often have a tremendous understanding of brand issues and the commercial imperatives of design. *Design for the 21st Century* is thereby not intended as a "chart-topping list". Rather, the aim has been to bring together a highly representative cross-section of the international contemporary design community, so as to present an in-depth, relevant and thought-provoking collection of projections on the key issues that will affect design and its possible course for the foreseeable future.

Of the designers included in this survey, it can be reasonably deduced that virtually all believe the primary goal of design is to make peoples' lives better. Design practice should respond – it seems to be agreed – to technical, functional and cultural needs and go on to create innovative solutions which communicate meaning and emotion and which ideally transcend their appropriate form, structure and manufacture. Given this commonality of purpose, however, when posed the question "What is your vision for the future of design?", their responses – outlined on the following pages – are remarkably varied. Among the many different concerns, issues and predictions which are articulated, however, several recurring themes come to the fore: the potential offered by new materials; the effect of new technology (computing, communications and industrial processes); the need for simplification; emotionalism (the psychological aspects of design); and the tendency towards either individualistic or universal solutions.

The increasing availability of new synthetic materials is broadly identified as one of the key motivational forces behind the emergence of new products – a trend that is forecast to continue well into the future. The culture of continuous development within the field of material science has led to a plethora of advanced materials that challenge our preconceived notions of how plastics, metals, glass and ceramics should behave under accustomed conditions. With the recent introduction of flexible ceramics, foamed metals, conductive light-emitting plastics and shape-memory alloys, for example, the most basic properties of materials are being turned on their head. In parallel with this, there is also a distinct trend towards the development and application of lightweight yet high tensile strength materials – from carbon-fibre to "floating" concrete – which are predicted to lead to either more expressive or essentialist forms. Synthetic polymers, which are increasingly able to mimic the properties of natural materials while also often possessing remarkable tactile qualities, have been shown in particular to be radically altering the formal potential of new products. Many of the designers included in this book are pioneering remarkable applications for materials such as these, as the product designs illustrated here demonstrate. But while most designers predict, like Jane Atfield, that "the integration of highly technological materials and processes will widen and become more accessible", others such as Emmanuel Dietrich have voiced concern that synthetics can sometimes be difficult to work with and are not always developed for their capacity to wear well.

New technologies – computers, communications and industrial processes – have in the last five years assisted enormously in the research and implementation of design, and are widely predicted to lead to increasingly miniaturized, multi-functional and better-performing products. More sophisticated CAD/CAM (computer-aided design/computer-aided manufacture) systems, RP (rapid prototyping) and aligned processes such as 3D stereolithography have considerably expedited the manufacture of smaller runs of products which are tailored more to meet individual needs. At the same time, these types of technologies are helping to streamline the design process from initial concept to working prototype. Today, computer-generated designs can be sent via ISDN lines directly to RP facilities and to manufacturers at the touch of a button. By ultimately accelerating the design process, these technologies are not only reducing front-end costs for manufacturers but are also providing designers with greater freedom for experimentation. CAD/CAM and its related technologies have already had a profound effect on product development, offering the designer the scope and flexibility to evolve exceptionally complex forms and to modify and customize products. Given the increasing potential for spawning a multiplicity of product variations, however, many of the featured designers agree with Jonathan Ive when he states that "our real challenge is to make relevant and extend technological capability."

Within the last five years, the Internet too has had a remarkable impact on the design process and has triggered, according to Lunar Design, "the move from mass production to mass customization". The freedom and ease of such communication technologies have also led to an ever-increasing transfer of design ideas and the cross-pollination of disciplines. This tendency towards integration is a result, too, of the increasing miniaturization of technology, which will undoubtedly continue unabated for the foreseeable future. Nano-technology has already led to the development of atomic-level mechanical components and will certainly play a significant role in the design of multi-functional "smart" products in the near to medium-term future. As the 21st century progresses, information technologies are widely expected to be incorporated into the design of products to such an extent that they will eventually be regarded as just another type of material – akin to glass or plastics – with which to develop innovative and better-performing solutions. Countering this vision of a brave new world of all-pervasive advanced technology, however, a few designers are promoting the use of low-tech processes that not only have a minimal impact on the natural environment, but also reject the insatiable demand for ever more product variety and volume.

In response to the current and predicted technological complexity of the 21st century, simplification has clearly become a key objective in design. Many of the designers included here concur strongly with the words of Alberto Meda: "Technology must be tamed in order to realize things that have the simplest possible relation with man – we must reject technologically driven industrial goods that have no regard for human needs and no communicative rationality." There can be little doubt that the future onus on designers will be to devise products that can be easily understood and used in an intuitive way. Similarly, the simplification of structural form – essentialism – will not only provide the means by which designers can gain the most from the least, but will also assist in the realization of forms that possess an inherent emotional purity. Simplification in design will thus both reduce the white noise of contemporary living and provide one of the best ways of enhancing the quality of products and, thereby, their durability.

The psychological aspects of design are also extensively addressed and given prominence as never before. There is a general consensus that products need to go beyond considerations of form and function if they are to become "objects of desire" in an increasingly competitive marketplace. To achieve this, products must make pleasurable emotional connections with their end-users through the joy of their use and/or the beauty of their form. Emotionalism is considered by many of the designers included here not only as a powerful and essential way of facilitating better and more meaningful connections between products and their users, but as an effective means of differentiating their solutions from those of their competitors. To this end, many designers, such as Ross Lovegrove, promote the use of soft, sensual, organic forms in an effort to provide their products with an emotionally seductive appeal. The innate tactility of such forms is deeply persuasive, even at a subconscious level. Cognitive of the fact that the emotional content of a design can determine its ultimate success, the general view among the majority of participating designers is that it is now as important to fulfil the consumer's desire for tools for loving as that for tools for living.

Of all the themes to emerge from the vision statements gathered here, the tendency towards either individualistic or universal solutions potentially holds the farthest-reaching consequences for the future direction of design. While some designers promote individualism in design as a channel for personal creative expression or to cater to consumer demand for individualistic products, others advocate universal solutions, which are generally more environmentally sound and whose emphasis upon greater functional and aesthetic durability offers better value for money. Individualism in design can be regarded as a reaction against the uniformity of mass production and, ultimately, the increasing homogenization of global culture. But with the objective of providing more expressive content, individualistic design solutions can often lead to higher costs and accelerated stylistic obsolescence. Given this, it is not surprising that, as an approach to design, individualism has hitherto generally remained in the realms of one-off and batch-manufactured products, rather than making serious inroads into large-scale industrial production. Although the individualism versus universality debate has raged since the earliest beginnings of Modern design practice, a fundamental paradox remains: while the nature of universal design solutions can sometimes be alienating, individualistic design solutions often remain the preserve of the wealthy élite. As has been discussed, however, new technologies are becoming widely available that would appear to be offering the means by which these two camps can be finally reconciled. The future of design may thus lie in the creation of universal solutions that can be efficiently adapted to meet individualistic needs.

The deliberation among the included designers on the appropriateness of individualistic versus universal solutions may well account for the relative absence of hypotheses on a unifying theory or new moral-philosophic basis of design. While many discuss the desirability of catering to the perceived need for greater individualism in design, for example, few comment on the future sustainability of such an approach, with its implications for increased waste production. Some designers, however, take an holistic view of current and longer-term concerns, and are in accord with the idea that when they create something, they are personally approving its existence and directing the fate of many resources. Certainly, there is a growing need for designers to view themselves as stakeholders in their product solutions and to develop them within an understanding of the environmental impact of every aspect of their manufacture, use and eventual disposal – from cradle to grave. But there is also a pressing requirement to connect consumers in more meaningful ways with technologically increasingly complicated products. To this end, it would seem that a more considered human-centric approach to design would provide the best means of satisfying both functional and psychological needs.

As designers clearly play a key role in determining the nature of manufactured products, there is little doubt that they can have an exceptional influence on the expectations and buying habits of consumers. There is consequently a growing moral imperative for them to chart a new and better direction in design, namely one which focuses on the development of real-need based, humanistic and sustainable solutions. By harnessing the advanced materials and technologies identified here while striving to provide simplified design solutions with an easier emotional connection for the consumer, designers should be able to create the types of ethical and relevant products that are needed for the future. The quality of our global material culture is being determined by the actions and choices we take now, and so it must be right that every individual – creator, maker and consumer – should acknowledge the need for a responsibility-based culture and should share in the collective goal of forging a better tomorrow.

CHARLOTTE AND PETER FIELL

Editors' note: We would like to express our immense gratitude to all those designers and design groups who have contributed to the successful realization of this unique project.

J Mays, **24.7 PickUp** concept vehicle
for Ford Motor Company, 2000

"Exciting, visionary and innovative design has always been the product of new materials and technology."

Werner Aisslinger

Werner Aisslinger, Studio Aisslinger, Oranienplatz 4, 10 999 Berlin, Germany
T +49 30 31 505 400 F +49 30 31 505 401 aisslinger@snafu.de www.aisslinger.de

"Design at the beginning of the 21st century will overcome the stylish minimalism of the last decade, with its innovation based purely on shape. Instead, there will be a return to parameters that have always been the basis of new epochs and dimensions in design: the sophisticated use of new materials and technologies. Historically, exciting, visionary and pioneering designs have always rested on the transformation of materials and technology into a new context. Today's lightning-speed technological advancements have led to the appearance of three-dimensional fibreglass, gels, aluminium foam, three-dimensional textiles and neoprenes from which entirely new products can be created. Aesthetically, the design of these future products will be utilitarian, organic, reduced, soft, puristic, poetic, modular and nomadic.
The products of the future will combine functional aspects with certain built-in event facilities. Eventually the act of experiencing products will become more important than functional or technical considerations and designers will have to be ever more sensitive to the dialogue between emotions and technology.
The distribution of products will also alter radically, with every object possessing a small chip that will allow you to order it directly. In this kind of future scenario, pure design quality will be a major decision factor for e-commerce consumers." WERNER AISSLINGER

1. **Plus Unit** trolley for Magis, 2000
2. ↓ **Juli** chair for Cappellini, 1998-2000

3
4
5

3.-4. **Soft** chaises longues for Zanotta, 2000
5. **Soft Cell** chair and stool (studio project – limited edition), 2000
6. **Cell-System** shelf for Zeritalia, 2000
7. **Endless Plastic** shelves for Porro, 1997-98 (permanent collection Die Neue Sammlung, Munich)
8. **Endless Plastic** panel for Porro, 1997-98

"Boredom is the mother of creativity."

Ron Arad

Ron Arad, Ron Arad Associates, 62, Chalk Farm Road, London NW1 8AN, England
T +44 20 7284 4963 F +44 20 7379 0499 info@ronarad.com www.ronarad.com

"In a slightly tongue-in-cheek press release for 'Not Made By Hand, Not Made in China', an exhibition of objects made by stereolithography and selective laser sintering (Milan 2000), I claimed that until recently there had been only four ways of making things. The process of making any object could be broken down into one or more of the following steps: WASTE (chip, carve, turn, mill, chisel – i.e. removal of excess material), MOULD (injection moulding, casting, rotation moulding, extruding etc. – i.e. pouring liquid material to take the form of its vessel when hardened); FORM (bending, pressing, hammering, folding, vacuum forming etc. – i.e. forcing sheet material into a shape), ASSEMBLE (bolting, gluing, riveting, soldering, welding etc. – i.e. joining parts together by any means), and, I went on to claim, there is now a fifth way – GROW, an object can be grown in a tank, layer by layer, by computer controlled laser beams.

Now I think all this can be reduced further – an object can be made by either ADDING or SUBTRACTING. Computers, with their ZEROS & ONES, love it. With CNC (Computer Numeric Control), RP (Rapid Prototyping), GM materials, and a little help from robotic friends, virtual can easily become actual; an image on screen rapidly transforms to a solid mass. There are virtually no limits. Smart materials, sharp tools, sci-fi production, it's all here. Now. " RON ARAD

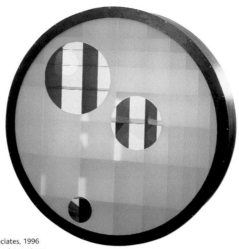

1. **RTW** shelves by Ron Arad Associates, 1996
2. ↓ **BOOP** coffee table by Ron Arad Associates
for Gallery Mourmans, 1998

3. ← **Tom-vac** stacking chairs for Vitra, 1997
4. **Victoria & Albert** chairs for Moroso, 2000
5. ↓ **Victoria & Albert** sofa for Moroso, 2000

"I am interested in the familiar elemental forms found in archetypes leading to simple and functional objects that evoke strong associations and narratives, often addressing environmental issues."

Jane Atfield

Jane Atfield, 244, Grays Inn Road, London WC1X 8JR, England
T +44 20 7278 6971 F +44 20 7833 0018 janeatfield@btinternet.com

"People will reject the dominance of consumerism and grow disillusioned with branding and materialism. As a result, shopping will lose its leisure and entertainment status and will be replaced by the Internet. The reduced demand for choice and possessions will be replaced with an emphasis on social experiences and better designed systems and communications.
Product designers will increasingly be motivated by meeting real needs and solving problems connected with children, older people, the disabled, single people and complicated families. An interactive process will develop with the designers acting as enablers and facilitators for the various groups' own ideas and requirements.
Moral and political factors will be important in determining what is developed and where, with localised solutions and low-tech resources becoming more important. Environmental concerns will increase in value over profit margins with, for example, materials, buildings and objects being routinely recycled. The integration of highly technological materials and processes will widen and become more accessible, controlling and regulating our environment to increasingly sophisticated levels." JANE ATFIELD

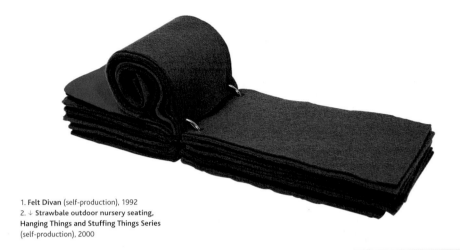

1. **Felt Divan** (self-production), 1992
2. ↓ **Strawbale outdoor nursery seating,
Hanging Things and Stuffing Things Series**
(self-production), 2000

3. ← **T-towels, Washing Up Series 1** for Up fabric, 2000 –
Sink, Bottles, Drainer & U-bend (designed in collaboration
with Robert Shepherd)
4. **Pillows Lounger** from **Hanging Things and Stuffing
Things Series** (self-production), 2000
5. **RCP2** chair for Made of Waste, 1993 – reissued in
monochrome recycled plastic derived from chopping
boards, 1998
6. **Amaretti** children's play trolley from **Biscuit Collection**
for Oreka Kids, 2000

"Simplicity and surprise, materiality and immateriality, from object to space."

Shin + Tomoko Azumi

Shin + Tomoko Azumi, Unit 7, Haybridge House, 15 Mount Pleasant Hill,
London E5 9NB, England
T +44 20 8880 0031 F +44 20 8880 0697 mail@azumi.co.uk www.azumi.co.uk

"In the future we hope that design will help us achieve a 'better life' rather than just 'better sales'. Between the 80's and early 90's, design became a tool for commercial marketing. That was not altogether a bad thing, but now we think it should be used to create a desirable environment and that greater emphasis should be placed on 'individuality' in the future. People will have more choice as quick communication and fast transportation make a wider range of designs from across the world accessible to them. In that situation, personal attachment will become a more important factor in design. Finally, for us, the future of design is an extended horizon of where we are and what we feel at the moment. It is not an entity in itself."

SHIN + TOMOKO AZUMI

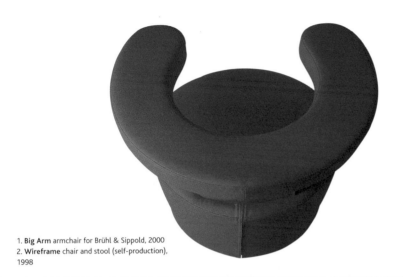

1. **Big Arm** armchair for Brühl & Sippold, 2000
2. **Wireframe** chair and stool (self-production), 1998

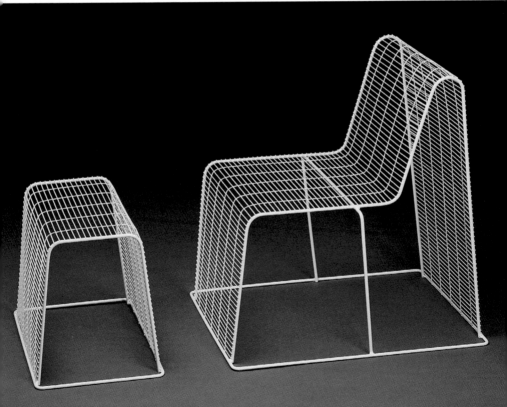

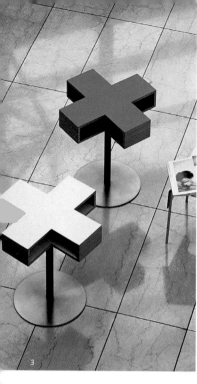

3. **Cross** tables for Trunk/Sumitomo Bakelite, 1999
4.-6. **Table=Chest** (self-production), 1995
7. **Keen Stand** at 100 % Design exhibition, London 2000 (with animation by Yuko Hirosawa)
8. **Music Tube** at Restir, Kobe 2000 (in collaboration with Noriyuki Ohtsuka)
9. **Stacking Chair** by Azumi for Kettle's Yard Gallery, 1998
10.-11. **H3** speaker and **HB-1** sub woofer for TOA, 2000

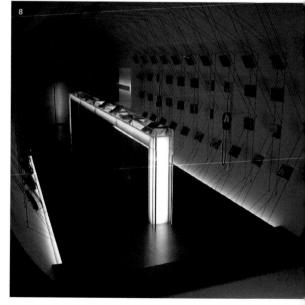

6

9

10

11

"I am happy with a design when it makes people smile."

Sebastian Bergne

Sebastian Bergne, 2, Ingate Place, London SW8 3NS, England
T +44 20 7622 3333 F +44 20 7622 3336 mail@sebastianbergne.com
also Via Bellombra 10, 40136 Bologna, Italy T/F +39 051 3395 609

"There are many ways an object can make someone smile: familiarity, surprise, beauty, satisfaction, pride, simplicity, humour or wonder.
If an object can stimulate this reaction whilst performing the function for which it was created, then it is well designed. It has in some way improved our lives. Design is the process by which these objects are created; it is not the object itself.
The future of design is the future of a way of thinking, a complex process of creativity that ultimately relies on the humanity of its audience to validate its existence. Designers always have and always will create for people's known or unknown needs and offer their solutions to new or age-old problems. Changes in society, technologies and materials alter the palette available to the designer to solve problems, but the process of creativity remains constant in its variety and unpredictability. In the end, however, the future of design is not in the hands of designers but rests on our ability to smile." SEBASTIAN BERGNE

1. **Kult** egg cup for WMF, 1999
2. ↓ **Torso** lamp for Authentics, 1996

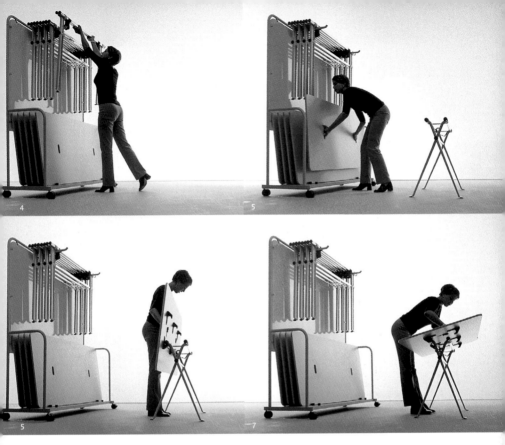

3. ← **Leg Over** stool for Authentics, 1997
4.-7. **IXIX** all-purpose table for Vitra, 1997
8. **Candloop** candlestick clip for
Wireworks UK, 1998

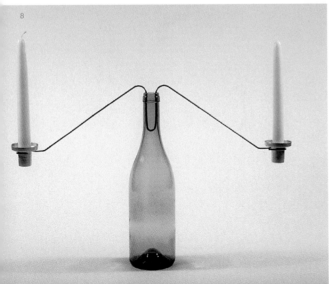

"Our work finds its characteristic in a diversity of approaches, from industry to craft, from the micro to the macro."

R. & E. Bouroullec

Ronan & Erwan Bouroullec, 51 Rue des Ursulines, 93200 Saint Denis, France
T/F +33 1 4 820 3660 bouroullec@wanadoo.fr

"We believe the future of design will tend towards a displacement of the fields of intervention. It will no longer rest solely on the question of the object or property, but rather on a harmony of situations, on a balanced personal ecosystem. In the future, production will be established around the properties/capacities of objects/people/the management of the tensions generated by a constant movement in life.

Liberated from the concept of the object, design will be generated by a more complex system which will involve an understanding of situations and a permanent freedom of movement. Objects/materials/sensitive devices (thermoregulated, lighter instead of heavier, etc.) are already able to accompany the human body in a responsive way. But, beyond the concept of emotions/ease of operation/comfort, it will be a question above all of a knowledge of the dialogues between an object, the various dimensions of its production and the user; where the individual efforts that have gone into its realization reflect a well-balanced ecosystem and an awareness of its development/history."

RONAN & ERWAN BOUROULLEC

1. **Square** vase for Cappellini, 1999
2. ↓ **Lis Clos** bed for Cappellini, 2000

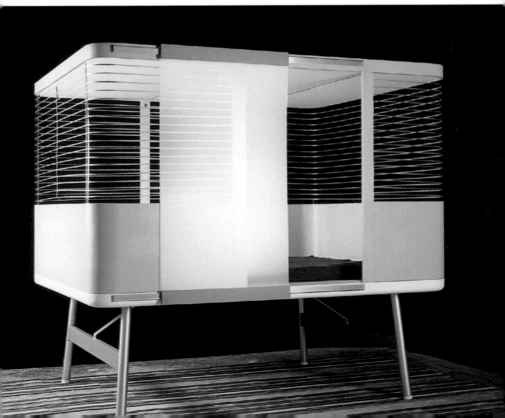

3. ← **Torique** ceramic collection for
Vallauris (limited edition), 1999
4. **Hole** lamps for Cappellini, 1999
5. **Vases Combinatoires Collection**
polyurethane vase for Galerie Néotu,
1997
6. **Vases Combinatoires Collection**
for Galerie Néotu, 1997
7. **Safe Rest** day-bed for Domeau &
Pérès, 1999

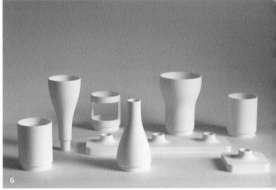

"The difference between good design and bad design is like the difference between a good story and a bad joke: one is worth hearing again and again; the other, preferably not!"

Julian Brown

Julian Brown, StudioBrown, 6, Princes Buildings, George Street, Bath BA1 2ED, England
T +44 1225 481 735 F +44 1225 481 737 Julian@studiobrown.com

"Like experience and culture, design reflects the times and technologies of today, but at its centre is a common purpose, namely to serve and assist man and to enable him to perform (physically and emotionally) within any of his chosen environments. This should not and probably never will change. Neither does the design process itself need to change; indeed, the intellectual and 'craft' roots of design remain as sound today as they ever were. It is undeniable that technology, computers and the web assist enormously in the research and implementation of new designs, but the brain, hands and feel of man will never be substituted. Indeed, I am confident that the more advanced our supportive technology becomes, the freer we will become to see clearly what we need or want to do and to find imaginative ways of getting there. Computers or machines (tools) will simply aid us. The designers who will contribute the most will be those who have never discarded these roots and who have the individuality, breadth and flexibility to practice their 'craft' within different enterprise cultures. Historically, this too will turn the tide in favour of the single or expert 'advisor' or 'designer', as was the case with Charles Eames and Herman Miller or Eliot Noyes at IBM. To conclude, while 'design' should ride the waves of technology (as master not mistress), unique and individual philosophies will become increasingly sought after and valued." JULIAN BROWN

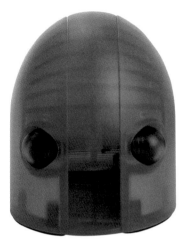

1.-2. **Hannibal** tape dispenser for Rexite, 1998

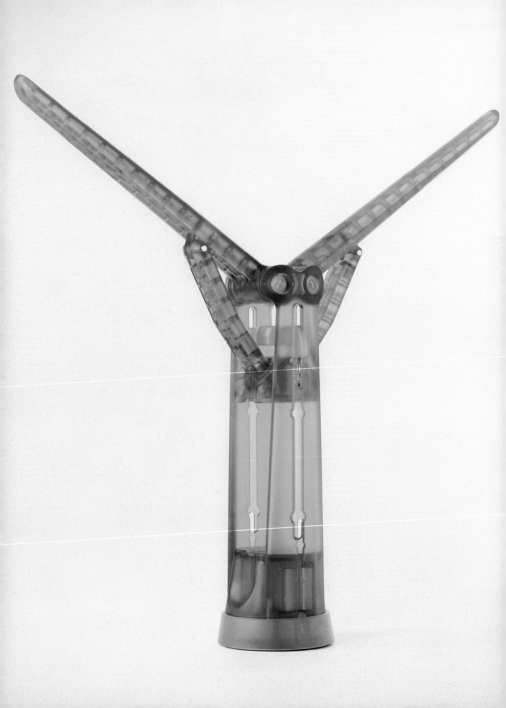

3. ← **Attila** beverage can compactor for Rexite, 1996
4.-5. **Isis** stapler for Rexite, 1999
6. **Titanum** cooking knives for Boker, 2000
7. **CD.2** cd storage system for Rexite, 2000

4

5

6

7

"We subvert the utility of materials so as to create in our objects a restless world of experimentation, creativity and innovation."

F. & H. Campana

Fernando & Humberto Campana, R. Barão de Tatuí 219, São Paulo SP, 01 226-030 Brazil
T +55 11 366 64152 F +55 11 382 53408 campanad@uol.com.br

"By experimenting with new materials, design in the future will be able to re-visit existent objects and subvert their functions into new 'destinations'. Sometimes, an established manufacturing technique can assist the development of new technologies for new projects as well as methods of recycling. Nowadays, we see a number of designers working individually in small studios, subverting the function of products to create new results. They may assemble parts or components of an existing object in such a way as to give it a new function or they may 'repeat' the same object in order to produce new textures. This is how we believe design will continue to grow creatively and take part in changing and extending our ways of living in this world.

The designer of the future should use references from his cultural background – traditions, colours, history – so that his products have an authenticity and originality that is not governed by fashion or global trends. These 'soul' references will help products communicate more directly. The future of design might be about allowing very imaginative projects with their own unique characteristics to play a part in the industrial scene so as to make life more creative and enjoyable – from 'canned-gassy' furniture that can be shaped into any form to folded houses inside envelopes that can be folded and unfolded any time any place to portable lamps that are powered by their own energy source inside crystal balls." FERNANDO & HUMBERTO CAMPANA

1. **Xingu** fruitbowl (self-production), 1998
2. ↓ **Tattoo** table for Fontana Arte, 2000

3

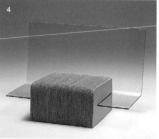

4

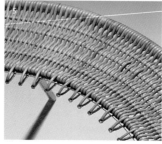

3. **Mixed Series** – Shark chair
(self-production), 2000
4. **Mixed Series** – Cardboard &
Polycarbonate chair for Hidden,
2000
5. **Mixed Series** – Shark chair
(detail) (self-production), 2000
6. → **Jenette** chair (self-
production), 2000

"It is the relationship between the object and its use, together with a capacity for ageing while increasing in value, that will deem an object classical."

Antonio Citterio

Antonio Citterio, Antonio Citterio & Partners, Via Cerva 4, 20 122 Milan, Italy
T +39 02 763 8801 F +39 02 763 88080 citterio@mdsnet.it

"I never use the word 'modern'. The concept of modernity implies an understanding of ancient things. I know this sounds like a paradox, but so it is. When expressing the tension found in my work, which is about the search for the 'spirit of the time', I use the word 'contemporary'. The contemporaneity of a design project includes and feeds the deep desire of anticipation. There is a perpetual shift between the anticipation of the project and the contemporaneity of the final product, which is the essence of my approach to design. I always try to design objects that are absolutely contemporary, exactly because they coincide perfectly with their time. The past years have seen a social evolution with the emergence of new technologies and new codes of communication, which have driven many designers to combine these elements in their own design, in a direct but unexplained way, within the stylistic parameters suggested by the computerization of design. I do not think, however, that this kind of design, which involves no pure formal effort, can lead to any substantial result. For me, the pertinence of the subject (without raising old questions of form and function) relies firstly on the ability to create clear and understandable objects and secondly on the ability to excite pleasure and the desire for ownership. I work like a hypothetical connoisseur of design, a man not so much interested in being surprised and deriving fun from an object but pursuing an interest in the precision of an object that is the result of an appropriate use of construction and detailing." ANTONIO CITTERIO

1. **Citterio 2000** cutlery for Hackman, 2000
2. ↓ **Web** armchairs for B&B Italia, 1998

3

4

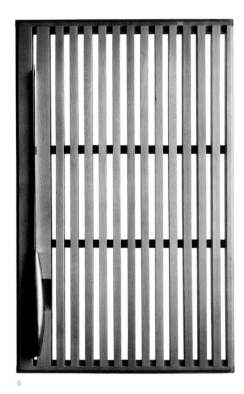

6

5

3. **Freetime** sofa for B&B Italia, 1999
4. **Freetime** chaise longue & sofa for B&B Italia, 1999
5. **H-Beam** lighting for Flos, 2000
6. **Citterio Collective Tools 2000** bread knife and cutting board for Hackman, 2000

"For me, design is ultimately about communicating ideas."

Björn Dahlström

Björn Dahlström, Dahlström Design, Frejgatan 20, 11349 Stockholm, Sweden
T +46 8 673 4200 F +46 8 673 4201 dahlstrom@dahlstromdesign.se

"Today we tend to work in separate cells, the designer on one side and the client on the other. Instead, we should build our systems on integrated thinking. The designer needs to be part of the industrial process, adopting the role of free-thinking catalyst. As a designer, I get a lot of inspiration moving from one type of the industry to another. I think design should have more influence on the engineering side of the development process. History shows that new materials and techniques have a direct effect on the evolution of design. I like to think that the designer in the future will be part of a research team trying to push frontiers forward: finding ways to help products and companies serve people better, creating more environmental friendliness, fine-tuning ergonomics, adapting existing materials and helping to develop new ones. Design is ultimately about communicating ideas. So if design in itself is going to evolve, designers will have to play a more central role in moulding the context in which the products are used."

BJÖRN DAHLSTRÖM

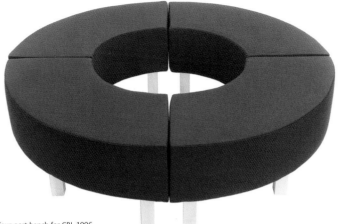

1. **BD-4** circular four-part bench for CBI, 1996
2. ↓ **Camper 3** tent for Fjällräven, 2000

3

4

3. **BD-1** easy chair for cbi, 1994
4. **Toycar** child's toy for Playsam, 1996
5. **Joystick** walking stick for Magis, 2000
6. **BD Relax** chaise for CBI, 2000
7. **BD3** candlestick for CBI, 1995
8. **Primus Powerjet** soldering torch for Primus, 1996

"Design always springs from an idea,
it is the form given to an idea."

Emmanuel Dietrich

Dietrich design, 24 rue des Belles Feuilles, 75116 Paris, France, T/F +33 1 44 05 15 39
e-mail: www@dietrich-design.com

"Ideas are transient and to be useful to us we have to give them physical form. A successful design is one that perfectly encapsulates the idea that inspired it. Each designer will interpret an idea in a different way, so that a finished design – whether colourful, sober, loud or baroque – reflects the character of the person who created it. Then there are practical considerations, technical limitations and commercial constraints. But despite these practicalities, there is always room for an infinite number of creative approaches. The process of design raises questions, and clients must be prepared for this, because each project should lead somewhere new.

I am fascinated by the technical challenges posed by design. The spatial relationships between different parts, their interdependence and the overall balance – I work and rework these aspects of a design, refining them until I am satisfied.

I love the possibilities inherent in different materials – natural materials, above all, are incredibly inspiring. Man-made materials never have quite the potential of organic ones, but new materials are coming closer to natural ones all the time and sometimes combine several of their qualities at once. These synthetics are not always easy to work with – they are usually developed for performance rather than appearance, texture or capacity to wear well – but they are constantly being improved, leading to new opportunities." EMMANUEL DIETRICH

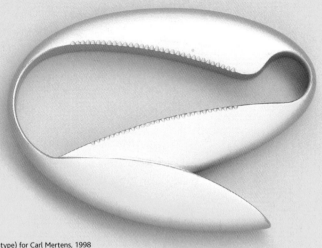

1. **Nutcracker** (prototype) for Carl Mertens, 1998
2. ↓ **Kettle** for Puiforcat, 1995

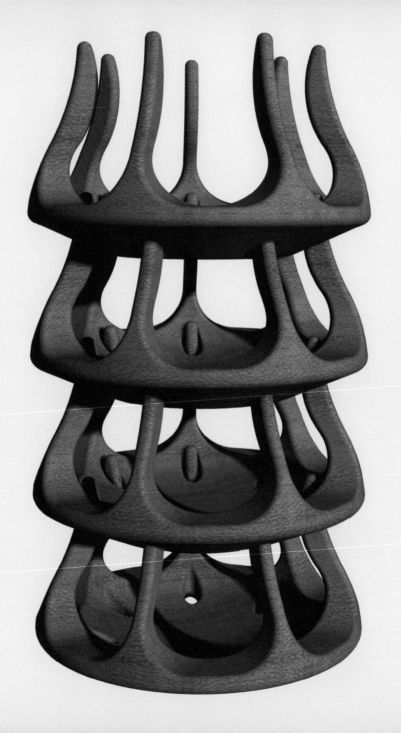

3. ← **Doumbia** stacking fruit boards for Meta Concept, 1999
4. **Watch** for Hermès, 1997
5. **Highlight** stacking candleholder for Ardi, 1999

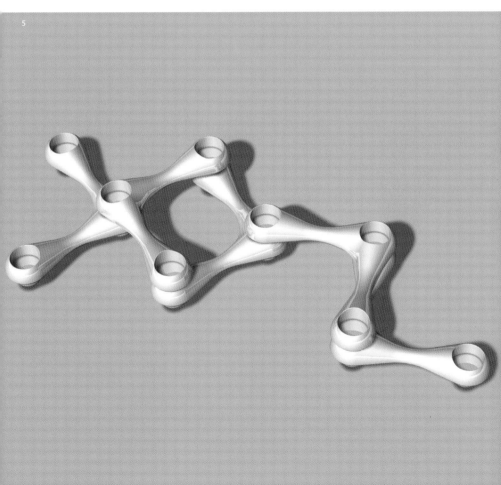

"Designing free of the constraints of mass production."

Elephant Design

Elephant Design, Nikko Akasaka Building 6F, 2-9-11 Akasaka Minato-ku, Tokyo 107-0052, Japan
T +81 3 5545 3061 F +81 3 5545 3062 www.elephant-design.com

"What is lacking in industrial design today? We could say it no longer provides a symbol of the future. Everywhere we look, we see designs that serve only to distinguish new models year by year. We rarely encounter a design that excites us just by looking at it, as was often the case in the sixties. On the other hand, the powerful imagination of architects and fashion designers is coming right across. What is the difference? The answer lies in whether or not one is allowed to design free of the constraints of mass production.

Taking up the challenge of this paradigm, we have found a solution in the Internet – gathering the ideas of artistic designers on our web site and then refining them through the opinion of consumers who visit the site. We bring people together who approve of certain design ideas and then begin looking for the right manufacturer. Once the number of orders reaches the volume required for a minimum lot, the consumer is then able to obtain what he or she 'really wanted'. In this way, artistic designers can present highly original designs to the public. The future could be bright for industrial design, as long as we don't feel the need to operate under the old dictates of mass production". ELEPHANT DESIGN

1. **Nuigurumi-kun** remote control
(self-production), 1999
2. ↓ Washing machine (concept study, designed
by Klein Dytham architecture), 1999

3.-4. **Cigarro** personal computer (limited production of 100 units), 2000
5. **TPF** compact fax machine, 1999
6. **Insipid** rice cooker (self-production), 1999
7. **Armadillo** cell-phone and information terminal (self-production), 2000

"A design that is not intentional, that has the freedom to offer a variety of appeals, can be discovered over the course of time spent with the object."

Naoto Fukasawa

Naoto Fukasawa, c/o IDEO Japan, AXIS Bldg. 4F, 5-17-1 Roppongi, Minato-ku, Tokyo 106-0032, Japan
T +81 3 5 570 2664   F +81 3 5 570 2669   naoto@ideojapan.co.jp   www.ideo.com

"Environment means the whole embodying the whole, but it tends to be perceived as if it exists outside of the self. Similarly, design is sometimes given an expression that assumes it will only be seen from the front. People often view an object or the environment as having a limited function, a single reason for being, but neither the environment nor the object should ever lose their immense potential for diversity. Scratching your forehead with a pencil or stacking documents on a chair are also ways of using these objects. Design can be seen as a process that not only accommodates the primary function of the object but also facilitates alternative functions that can be discovered within the object's active environment." NAOTO FUKASAWA

1. **Kinetic** watch for Seiko, 1997
2. ↓ **Message Watch** for Seiko, 1997

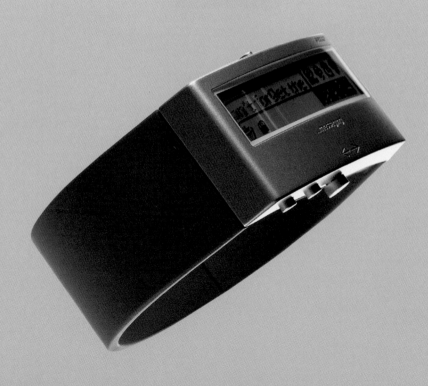

3. ← **Without Thought** cd player for DMN, as part of **Without Thought** project, 1990 manufactured and distributed by Muji
4.-5. **Tile** light for INAX, 1998
6. **Printables** printer for Epson, 1998
7. **New Domestic Cooking Tools** kettle for Matsushita, 1998

"I try to break the usual codes in order to pursue new emotions."

Jean-Marc Gady

Jean-Marc Gady, 52 Rue des Abbesses, 75 018 Paris, France
T/F +33 1 46 06 81 34 jmgady@club-internet.fr

"As an industrial and furniture designer, I have several work 'axes': for the most part my production is dedicated to 'typological' and functional research. According to my creative process, when I make up my mind to take on a project (whether a vase or a vacuum cleaner), I try to forget its aesthetic past and instead experiment using a 'virgin' eye so as to apprehend the object in other ways. Interaction is also a recurring theme in my approach to design. For me, it is important that the product become part of the user's evolution without complications of any kind. I think that nowadays, a designer has to be deeply impregnated by his time, catching every sign floating around. The designer needs to be a sharp observer so that he can accumulate enough 'matter' to mix with his personality so as to anticipate new patterns of consumption. Even so, there are no rules in design." JEAN-MARC GADY

1. **Moods** chaise longue for VIA project, 2000
2. ↓ **Air Cup** coffee cups for Ligne Roset, 2000

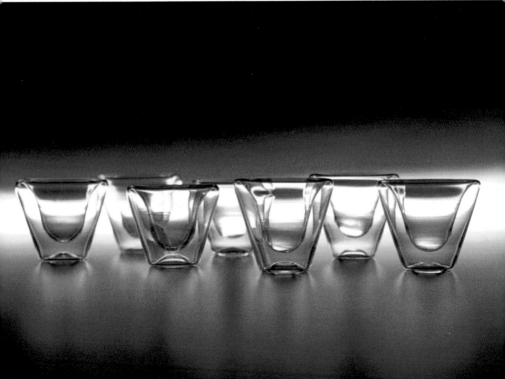

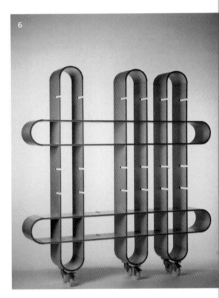

3. ← **La Chose** ashtrays for G2, 2000
4. **Submarine** vase for Cinna, 2000
5. **Punch-Light** for Project G2, 2000
6. **Isis** shelves for En Attendant Les Barbares project, 1997

"Moving to an emotional supermarket."

Stefano Giovannoni

Stefano Giovannoni, Giovannoni Design srl, Via Gulli 4, 20 147 Milan, Italy
T +39 02 487 03495 F +39 02 487 01141 studio@stefanogiovannoni.com
www.stefanogiovannoni.com

"Objects are not beautiful or ugly but are either suited or not to their time. Through their image and the technology used to produce them they communicate particular values that become part of our culture. To communicate through objects means telling a story of something that relates to life through a warm sensorial appeal connected with our memory and imaginary world.

The designer is increasingly involved in marketing concepts and technology. He cannot simply 'design' objects but must now shift his goals towards design strategies. The field of action is no longer that of the object but a hypothesis of comprehensive development for the product/company. This means putting strategies linked to communication, marketing and technology at the core of one's work. The public's needs and desires evolve rapidly – so it is necessary to take in these transformations all the time, while delivering loud and clear your personal view of the world.

I have asked myself many times whether we really need new products. Everybody in a developed society is in possession of the objects that answer every functional need. But to create wealth, companies have to produce in larger and larger quantities – on the one hand we have no need for new products, but on the other hand we must develop a new virtual system in order to anticipate the new and increasingly sophisticated fictional architecture of our desires. " STEFANO GIOVANNONI

1. **Big Bubbles** soap dish for Alessi, 1999
2. ↓ **Big Switch** lamp for Segno, 1996

3. ← **Magicbunny** toothpick holder for
Alessi, 1998
4. **Bombo** chair for Magis, 1999

"When I design, I design for people,
not for an abstract entity, a market,
but for real people, people I know,
people I love."

Konstantin Grcic

Konstantin Grcic, Konstantin Grcic Industrial Design, Schillerstrasse 40, 80 336 Munich, Germany
T +49 89 550 79995 F +49 89 550 79996 mail@konstantin-grcic.com
www.konstantin-grcic.com

"One principal experience from the past will clearly be determining our
future: the evolution of life (and this affects design) is conditioned by
the irrevocable loss of an absolute truth. We have had to learn that life
on our planet is not built around a single interpretation but rather
allows for many different interpretations simultaneously. Two sup-
posedly contradictive systems do not necessarily have to cancel each
other out. Future will therefore not produce one formula for design.
There will be no truth about what is good and what is bad design.
Something that a short time ago seemed reassuring and clear, might
suddenly raise queries and doubt. Something that has been unnoticed,
might suddenly bear an unexpected potential of beauty and interest.
The fragility in our existing conception of the world order guarantees
to be a permanent source of inspiration."

KONSTANTIN GRCIC

1. **Chef** microwave concept study for
Whirlpool, 2000
2. ↓ **Belle & Bon** egg-cup and spoon for
Porzellan-Manufaktur Nymphenburg, 1999

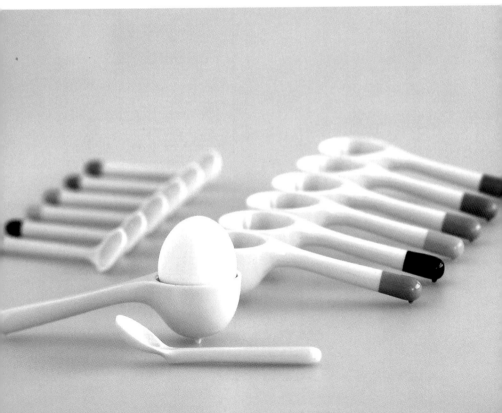

3. ← **Chaos** chair for ClassiCon, 2001
4. **Hertz** halogen light for Flos, 2000
5. **Scolaro** stool & table for Montina, 2000
6. **Relations** glassware for littala, 1999

"The less you see the designer's effort in the work, the better – effort should not be a visual commodity; it's simply a means to an end."

Sam Hecht

Sam Hecht, c/o Industrial Facility, Pegasus House, 2nd Floor, 116–120 Golden Lane, London ECIY OTF, England, T +44 207 253 3234 F +44 207 490 4411
sam@industrialfacility.co.uk www.industrialfacility.co.uk

"Design continues to face a dilemma when determining what portion of a product should be developed to be chosen in the shop, and what portion of it should be developed to be used. In an educational model, design is produced according to use, and a product's popularity is measured by how successfully it does its job. But in the shop model, working well is simply not enough. The product needs to be selected and purchased in an arena where many products, from different manufacturers, work just as well. This has led to a situation where saturated markets require the 'choosing' to be more important than the 'using'. Products have become their own embodiment of branding. If I am to design, must I relinquish the using for the choosing? Like the phrase 'things become second nature', we do not need to see what we are doing to achieve a result. Form is a mechanism for use, rather than an aesthetic (or a surface upon which choice is played out). It is something that needs to be evolved and not applied. The simplicity of tools illustrates this idea: their simplification results from complex cultural production. The question 'shall we design a beautiful hammer or a plain hammer?' is absurd. And there is no reason why a computer or a television is not thought of in the same way. The future needs to be simplistic, if we are to consume technology, where the illustration of complexity is of no importance, but only the result. Form will become mechanical, with its roots in the ordinary. As projects involve an ever-greater complexity, the more resonant the truth needs to be." SAM HECHT

1. **Rice** cooker for Matsushita, 1997
2. ↓ **Water faucet** and control for INAX, 1998

3. ← **Soft Wrist** phone for ElekSen
(limited edition), 1999–2000
4. **Airbus A380** window for
Airbus Industrie, 2000
5. **Post-It** e-mail watch for
Seiko Communications, 1997
6. **Watercycle Pavilion** for
Thames Water, 2000
7. **LG** dishwasher for LG Electronics,
2000

"The future of design is seduction."

Matthew Hilton

Matthew Hilton, The Hamlet, Champion Hill, London SE5 8AW, England
T +44 20 7501 8585 F +44 207501 8381 matthew.hilton@virgin.net

"Stanley Kubrick's 2001: A Space Odyssey, made over thirty years ago, had the fantastic future edge that makes the latest amorphic shapes on the pages of today's design magazines look like has-beens. The reality of the brave new world of communications technology has had far-reaching implications within the globalization of economics and business, but this has had little impact on the domestic interior. The dominant design theory of the 20th century was fuelled by modernism with its roots firmly based in manufacturing and social issues. The proliferation of computer technology at the end of the last century and its enormous influence on design education has naturally had a strong impact on the shape of design today. Its positive influence can be seen in the growth of virtual links between design and manufacturing.
I feel that we are going through a crisis in design dealing with this transitional period which marks a shift away from modernism and in turn embraces technology, retailing, marketing and, of course, branding. In terms of design developing in parallel with the production of man-made materials and manufacturing techniques, we are only paying lip-service to these developments and realistically we are not living very differently than we were fifty years ago. The gadgets are there but in terms of form we definitely owe more to the Eameses that any other figures at the turn of the century." MATTHEW HILTON

1. **Havana** armchair for SCP, 2000
2. ↓ **Jammy Dodger** children's desk
from Biscuit Collection for Oreka Kids, 2000

3. ← **Wait** chair for Authentics, 1998
4. **Mercury** sofa for Driade, 1997
5. **Voyager** chair for Driade, 1997
6. **Presshound** bookcase & magazine rack
for SCP, 1997
7. **Easy Chair** for SCP, 1995

4

5

6

7

"Design is about creatively exploiting constraint."

Inflate

Inflate, 11, Northburgh Street, London EC1V 0AN, England
T +44 20 7251 5453 F +44 20 7250 0311 info@inflate.co.uk www.inflate.co.uk

"We specialise in developing projects around old, under-exploited manufacturing processes. Initially all our designs were inflatable and used high-frequency welding processes. By 1997 we had added dip moulding to our portfolio, and in 2000 our first rotational moulded products were launched. We use our own branded products as a way of commercially experimenting with manufacturing processes and illustrating the potential of our work. Alongside our branded products, we like to surprise the client with ingenious gimmicks ranging from small promotional invitations to portable architecture.
Everyone wants to make history in some sort of way. We want to make an impact, but you won't if you do the same things as everyone else. Our priority is coming up with something new, not just capitalizing on what we've already done. To be known as a source of inspiration, we need to keep moving along, and for this we've set up 'The Shed' – a separate unit for the generation of new ideas and principles that will enable us to continue selling surprise at no extra cost." INFLATE

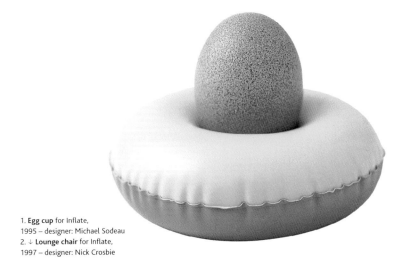

1. **Egg cup** for Inflate,
1995 – designer: Michael Sodeau
2. ↓ **Lounge chair** for Inflate,
1997 – designer: Nick Crosbie

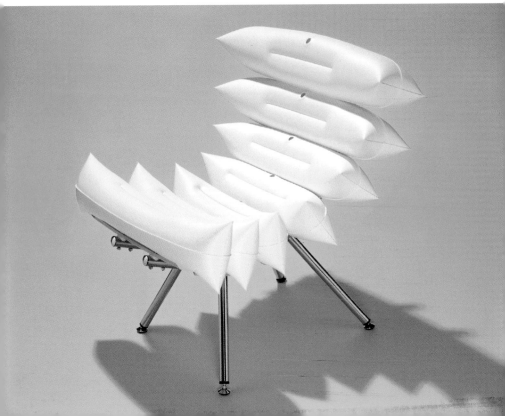

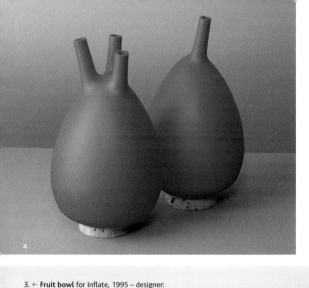

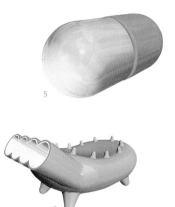

3. ← **Fruit bowl** for Inflate, 1995 – designer:
Nick Crosbie
4. **Mr & Mrs Prickly** salt and pepper shakers
for Inflate, 1997 – designer: Nick Crosbie
5. **Lozenge** storage capsule for Inflate, 2000 –
designer: Inflate Studio
6. **Soap lounger** soap and toothbrush holder
for Inflate, 2000 – designer: Inflate Studio
7. **MEMO** bean bag for Inflate, 1999 – designers:
Inflate & Ron Arad

"Always question why you are doing something, unless you are being paid a ridiculous amount of money, then really question it."

James Irvine

James Irvine, Via Sirtori 4, 20 129 Milan, Italy
T +39 02 295 34532 F +39 02 295 34534
james@james-irvine.com www.james-irvine.com

"The classic role of designers is destined to change in the near future. The recent 'style wars' will of course carry on and become more and more sophisticated. However, industry and designers alike are becoming aware that it's all getting a bit pointless. Even consumers are starting to wise up. They are beginning to question the fundamental necessity of all these things: 'Do I need to spend thousands of pounds on a car then sit in a traffic jam? Perhaps I don't need a car. But the problem is how do I replace it?'
I have the feeling many products are designed in steps by people who don't talk to each other – specialists blinkered by their own speciality. Basic issues are rarely discussed. I am sure a new breed of thinkers will become relevant to industry. They will not be designers but people capable of connecting different disciplines to bring a new relevance to products whether ecological or social. I am looking forward to the day when my relationship with industry will be participating in such thinking. Of course in the meantime, I am quite willing to discuss the finer points of the radii on the leg of my next chair." JAMES IRVINE

1. **Soundwave** microwave & radio for Whirlpool, 2000
2. ↓ **Üstra** city bus (Hanover) for Mercedes Benz, 1999

3. **Earth planters** for Arabia, 2001

"Vision is not only a founding idea but necessarily the resolution to ensure its realization."

Jonathan Ive
AND THE DESIGN TEAM

Apple Computer Inc., Industrial Design,
20 730, Valley Green Drive, Cupertino, California, 95 014 USA
T + 408 996 1010 www.apple.com

"An object exists at the meeting of technology and people. As designers we not only influence the nature of that meeting but by creating something physical we have a potent and immediate means of communicating the identity and very meaning of an object.
Far from designing enclosures around anonymous albeit powerful logic boards, our real challenge is to make relevant and extend technological capability. Searching for wholly new approaches to product configuration and manufacturing requires the development of fundamentally new materials and processes.
Significant solutions tend to emerge when new production technologies are exploited as a means to a greater end; the crafting of objects that stand testament to people rather than manufacturing or functional imperatives." JONATHAN IVE

1. **iSub** subwoofer for Harman Kardon, 1999
2. ↓ **Power Mac G4** computer for Apple Computer, 1999

3.-4. **Apple Cinema Display** 22" flat panel for
Apple Computer (front and side views), 1999

"Identifying the opportunity and creating the 'idea' for each and every project that will actively inspire others to believe that even the improbable is possible."

Jam

Jam Design and Communication Ltd., 4th Floor, 35-39, Old Street,
London EC1V 9HX, England
T +44 20 7253 8998 F +44 20 7253 9966 all@jamdesign.co.uk www.jamdesign.co.uk

"In effect, design is about asking questions and finding new opportunities. Design will gain in social and economic significance as it continues to create platforms for new experiences. It will explore different ways to communicate, integrate and ultimately relate to what surrounds us. It will bring new values of responsibility, sustainability and commitment to a society driven by economics. Design will also stimulate the conception of new products or ideas, enabling new activities to emerge or eliminating unwanted ones.
We feel people are now in an exciting period of cultural change that requires a new way of thinking – as the pace and style of life changes, people will think and communicate in new ways. This is what excites us and it is where we fit in. We want to pioneer a new attitude between our clients and their market audience. By focusing on the use of design and conceptual projects to build and communicate brands, our clients benefit from the internal and external effects of these projects, which act as a catalyst to innovation, change and increased opportunity." JAM

1. **Ringos** napkin ring designed in collaboration
with Zotefoams Plc (produced by Jam), 1997
2. ↓ **Panel** light designed in collaboration with
Zotefoams Plc (limited edition by Inflate), 2000

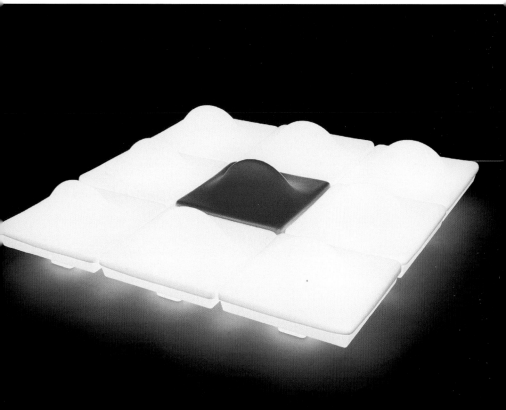

3. **2020 Vision** showing Corus Concept car for Corus, 2000, in cooperation with Softroom
4. **Foam Dome** designed in collaboration with Zotefoams (produced by Jam), 1998
5. **Three-door** concept washing machine for Whirlpool, 1999

6. **Concept kitchen** for Whirlpool and Corian (shown at 100 % Design exhibition), 1999, in cooperation with Softroom and Linbeck Rausch

"The fundamental purpose of design is to either answer or formulate essential questions."

Harri Koskinen

Harri Koskinen, c/o Hackman Designor Oy Ab, Iittala Glass, 14 500 Iittala, Finland
T +358 204 39 6318 F +358 204 39 6303 harri.koskinen@designor.com

"I'm writing about the future of design, my future and the future of us all. At present, I'm working as a designer of consumer goods under commission from companies that produce them. The designs I create are meant for everyday use in the near future. When commissioning work from me, companies outline a situation envisioned for the near future: what the consumer needs and is allowed to need. The problems are very realistic, involving improvements to the products that are available now as well as new perspectives. My interest in my work lies in insights, in the moments when I figure out a solution that leads to products that are more functional and easier to manufacture.

In the future, we'll occupy the now more than we do at present. The things we win for ourselves will give us more to fight for. We evolve a new consciousness by searching for it. The fulfilling of basic needs remains the most important activity. Over the ocean, there might still be arable fields to farm.

Design plays a part in all of this – but, on the other hand, it is also very far removed from it. In the future, we'll give more thought to the future." HARRI KOSKINEN

1. **Tools** outdoor cooking utensils for
Hackman, 2000
2. ↓ **Block** lamp for Design House
Stockholm, 1998

3

4

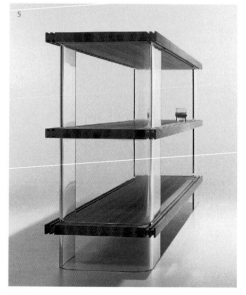

5

6

7

3. **Air** food container for Arabia, 2001
4. **Slow** lamp (one-off), 2000
5. **Shelf** system (prototype), 2000
6. **Atlas** candleholder & vase for Iittala, 1996
7. **Alue** bowls for Pro Arte Collection, Iittala, 2000

"It's only the future if it can't be made."

Ross Lovegrove

Ross Lovegrove, Studio X, 21, Powis Mews, London W11 1JN, England
T +44 20 7229 7104 F +44 20 7229 7032 studiox@compuserve.com

"We are entering a unique era of re-evaluation of ourselves and our habitat. We have reached a level of confidence in our creative abilities that is fuelling an unprecedented level of inquiry in all fields, from genetic engineering to fuel cells and medicine to the abstract depths of our organic universe. The process by which we are discovering new possibilities is being rapidly accelerated by computing technology – a technology that we always knew would open our minds. Indeed, it is this concept of inevit-ability that intrigues me especially when applied to the world we see and touch ... our physical world. As boundaries blur, this world will become stranger and less predictable – a fabulous prospect for those of us who believe that strangeness is a consequence of innovative thinking. The irony of all this is that ultimately, creativity generated by such soup-like freedom will lead mankind full circle back to nature, its organic composition, its purpose and with it forms that will no longer be limited by man's imagination.

Organic design comes from organic thinking. It moves people from the inside out, stimulating deep primordial resonances that transcend superficial trends. So far we have only been guessing, but the enduring beauty of the organic works of art produced by the likes of Henry Moore and Frei Otto tends to suggest that the combination of raw intuition combined with a degree of cellular, fractal logic will inevitably begin to greatly influence the form and physicality of our man-made world." ROSS LOVEGROVE

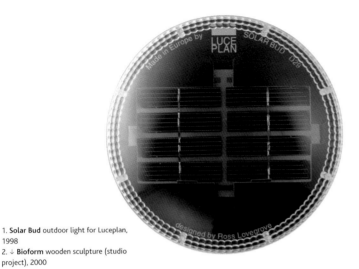

1. **Solar Bud** outdoor light for Luceplan, 1998
2. ↓ **Bioform** wooden sculpture (studio project), 2000

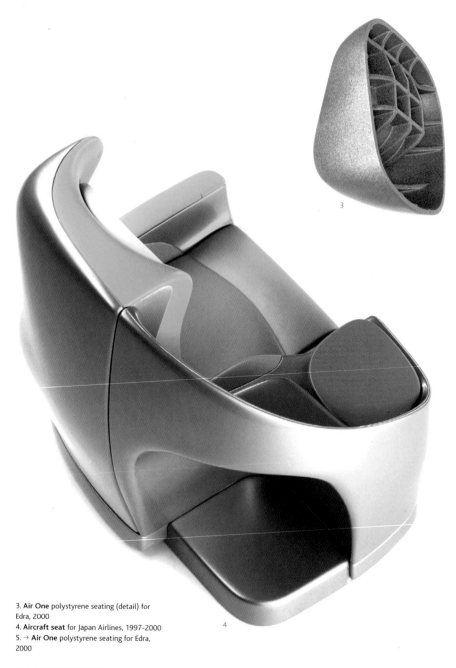

3. **Air One** polystyrene seating (detail) for
Edra, 2000
4. **Aircraft seat** for Japan Airlines, 1997-2000
5. → **Air One** polystyrene seating for Edra,
2000

"Our goal is to solve business problems by connecting brand, technology and people in innovative and compelling ways."

Lunar Design

Lunar Design, 537, Hamilton Avenue, Palo Alto, California 94 301, USA
T + 650 326 7788 F +650 326 2420 info@lunar.com www.lunar.com

"In just a few years, the Internet has revolutionized the way the world does business. It has already triggered the move from 'mass production' to 'mass customization'. In fact, almost anyone with a product idea can sell goods directly over the Web. Entrepreneurs don't have to wait for a retailer to carry their products. And consumers are no longer limited to merchandise that stores have in stock. For product designers, mass customization presents a compelling challenge: to develop flexible products and modular systems that give consumers meaningful choices.

Just as technology is becoming increasingly transparent and compact, the purpose of products is becoming increasingly comprehensive. The size and appearance of tomorrow's products will, more and more, reflect their ability to deliver a service, to inform consumers of their brand's benefit proposition, and to reflect customers' preferences. Indeed, connecting people to technology in easy and engaging ways will become the primary way to differentiate a brand.

Designers today carry a great responsibility. They must create products that communicate a brand promise, that are efficient to manufacture at high quality levels, and that resonate strongly with the people who will buy and use them. Future products will soon have to be more ecologically friendly, too. This need is particularly important as consumer markets emerge in developing countries, further straining natural resources." LUNAR DESIGN

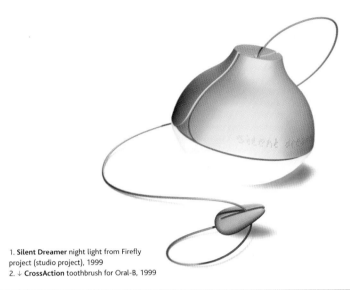

1. **Silent Dreamer** night light from Firefly
project (studio project), 1999
2. ↓ **CrossAction** toothbrush for Oral-B, 1999

3. ← **HP Pavilion FX70** flat panel display for Hewlett Packard, 1999
4. **HMD-A200, FD Trinitron** monitor for Sony, 1999
5. **Daisy Glow** night light from Firefly project (studio project), 1999
6. **Travel Tote** from *Service-as-Product* range (studio project), 1998
7. **PoP** night light from Firefly project (studio project), 1999

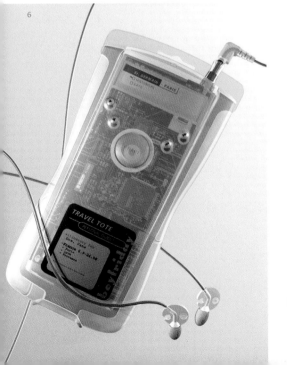

"Form is what is there – not what seems to be there; therefore, we must speak in terms of the work that brings it into being."

Enzo Mari

Enzo Mari, Enzo Mari e Associati, Piazzale Baracca 10, 20 123 Milan, Italy
T +39 02 481 7315 F +39 02 469 3651

"The original power of design to create a utopia must be recovered. If this is the allegory of the potential transformation, the message must reach as many people as possible. The people who are aware that our environment is being alienated, must continue as leaders in its transformation. At present, mechanisms driven by the information revolution will swallow any idea that is vomited up in the form of merchandise. Over the coming decades, the first requirement will be to discover suitable approaches capable of isolating the idea of transformation from superfluous issues. To do this, the ideal concept will have to be distinguished from all those generated by irresponsible anarchies, which reject or trivialize the impulse towards utopia and in so doing render any involvement of the people impossible. In the meantime, it would be well worth the effort to promote a general acceptance of the principle that 'ethics must guide all design' (a code similar to the Hippocratic Oath)." ENZO MARI

1. **Alta Pressione** pressure cooker for
Zani e Zani, 1998
2. ↓ **Ypsilon** table for Magis, 1999

3. ← **Miss Tea** pot and warmer for Leonardo, 1998
4. **Sigmund** daybed for Arte e Cuoio, 1999
5. **Elastica** fruit bowl for Zani e Zani, 1999
6. **Dama** pouf for Arte e Cuoio, 1999

"Every new product development must contain innovation."

J Mays

J Mays, c/o Product Development Center, Ford Motor Company,
20 901 Oakwood Blvd., Dearborn MI 48 124-4077, USA
T +313 621 6089 F +313 845 1119 media@ford.com www.media.ford.com

"I believe that good design rests on three elements: simplicity, credibility and the aspirations of the customer. The task for a designer is to create a design that communicates the nature of the product, connects emotionally with the customer and, on a good day, expands the vocabulary of the genre. It's a relatively easy philosophy to articulate – a bit more complicated to execute.

Communicating the nature of the product, for example, means more than reflecting what the product does – its function. It also includes credibly communicating the character of the product – its integrity, the essential qualities it represents and the brand promise – in short, the critical attributes that uniquely distinguish the product. Too often we seem to be peeking at each other's drawing boards rather than searching out new ways of communicating with the customer. As a result, we cycle through periods when everybody's work looks the same.

I see two remedies for this. First, we need a willingness to explore new ideas of what a product could look like based on other important things in the customer's lifestyle. Second, we need to recognize that design does not communicate through shape alone. The more senses we engage the stronger the product experience.

As to the future, the more complicated our culture becomes, the more we will value simple, credible design messages that engage our emotions and reflect our aspirations." J MAYS

1.-2. **24.7 Wagon** concept vehicle (interior and voice-activated reconfigurable projected image display) for Ford Motor Company, 2000

3.-4. ← **(My) Mercury** concept vehicle
(opening-back rear doors) for Ford Motor
Company, 1999
5. **24.7 PickUp** concept vehicle for Ford Motor
Company, 2000

"The attempt to achieve simple things meets what you might call a 'biological' need for simplicity. Since we are complicated beings, let us at least be surrounded by simple objects."

Alberto Meda

Alberto Meda, Via Savona 97, 20 144 Milan, Italy
T +39 02 422 90157 F +39 02 477 16169 a.meda@planet.it

"The design process is not linear, it is rather a complex activity similar to a game's strategy, but strangely it is a game where the rules are continuously changing and that is what makes it so fascinating and mysterious. Technology widens the scope of knowledge, but it is necessary to understand that technological development must no longer proceed without justification.

Technology must be tamed in order to realize things that have the simplest possible relation with man – we must reject technologically driven industrial goods that have no regard for human needs and no communicative rationality. Technology is not an end in itself, but a means of producing simple things capable of enhancing expressively the space around them. Paradoxically, the more complex technology becomes, the better it can generate objects with a simple, unitary, 'almost organic' image.

Design should be seen as a strategy that fishes in the realms of technological fantasy. Its purpose is not to conjure up an image that emphasizes scientific and technical thinking, and therefore technology for its own sake, but to use technology as a means of aesthetic-figurative interpretation and exploration of possible performances. I feel the necessity to produce things with a recognizable cultural quality – things that make 'sense', in addition to 'shape'. In other words, design should be approached with a view to making products capable of solving unsolved problems." ALBERTO MEDA

1. **Floating Frame** chair for Alias, 2000
2. ↓ **Fortebracco** task lamp for Luceplan
(designed with Paolo Rizzatto), 1998

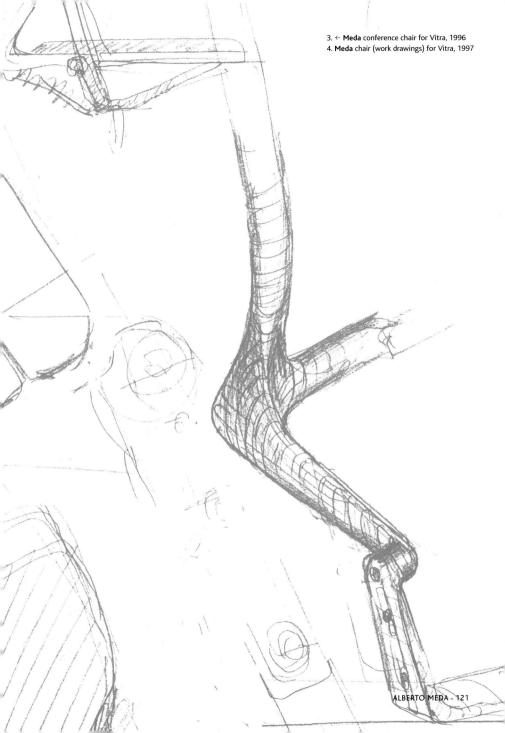

3. ← **Meda** conference chair for Vitra, 1996
4. **Meda** chair (work drawings) for Vitra, 1997

"Keep a thing for seven years and you'll find a use for it." (IRISH PROVERB)

Jasper Morrison

Jasper Morrison, Office for Design

"There are many possible futures of design, but let's imagine an ideal one first. Design (the real thing) gradually saturates all areas of industry bringing exceptional aesthetic and material quality to products, which can be marketed at affordable levels, enriching our daily lives beyond imagination. And now a less desirable future: marketing people take over industry and saturate it with their idea of design (not the real one), flooding the world with useless articles that nobody needs, which can only be bought as gifts for others. As usual, the future lies somewhere between these extremes." JASPER MORRISON

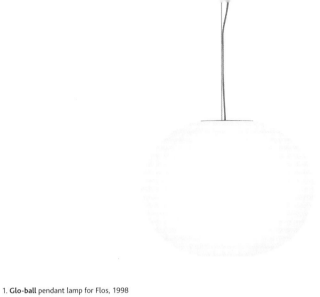

1. **Glo-ball** pendant lamp for Flos, 1998
2. ↓ **Three** sofa for Cappellini, 1992

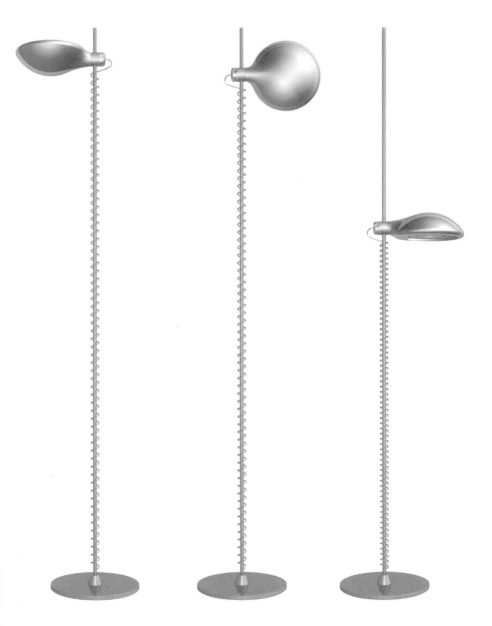

"I approach design in a fairly subliminal way, which is lucky because I don't have time to think about it too much ..."

Marc Newson

Marc Newson, Marc Newson Ltd., 1, Heddon Street, London W1R 7LE, England
T +44 20 7287 9388 F +44 20 7287 9347 pod@marc-newson.com www.marc-newson.com

"Without doubt, design will play a more important role in our lives in the future whether we like it or not. Certainly, it will play a much bigger role in large companies. In a sense, it's as if design is being re-born as we speak, strangely coinciding with the new millennium. As well, I suppose the word 'design' will become increasingly familiar to most people. My hope is that it will not simply become a commercial catch-phrase, but come to define something that implies quality and improvement." MARC NEWSON

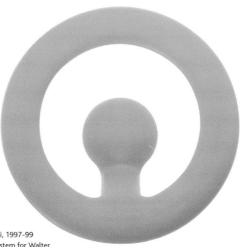

1. **Sygma** clothes hook for Alessi, 1997-99
2. ↓ **W. & L.T.** retail shelving system for Walter
Van Beirendonck, 1996-97

3. ← **W. & L. T.** retail shelving system for
Walter Van Beirendonck, 1996-97
4. **Orgone** plastic chair for Pod, 1998
5. **Bath Plug** for Alessi, 1997
6. **David Gill** chair for B&B Italia, 1998

"Our design aspirations: surprise, beauty, invention, curiosity, intelligence and joy."

PearsonLloyd

Luke Pearson & Tom Lloyd, PearsonLloyd, 42 -46, New Road, London E1 2AX, England
T +44 207 377 0560 F +44 207 377 0550 mail@pearsonlloyd.co.uk www.pearsonlloyd.co.uk

"We present an 'industrial' design, which entertains and encourages cultural and technological cross-pollination by working across diverse scales, technologies and functions. This comes from a love of materials and processes and how things are put together. By working across different industries and processes that are not 'ours', we can play and experiment, never becoming slaves to the traditional understanding of how those materials 'should' go together. Working in varied areas of design allows an exchange of ideas either in terms of cultural ideas or in terms of language and technology.

The spectrum of design for manufacture exists from craft to mass production. Our design work attempts to place objects appropriately and sympathetically within this spectrum, as a response to both technological and cultural needs. This also relates to a responsibility within the perceived global economy, to design sustainable goods within a sustainable system.

Our aim is to provide objects that express or relay meaning and emotion and go beyond their appropriate form, structure and manufacture. Our desire is to avoid subscribing to dogma or fashion and to create innovative rather than archetypal objects that are universally understandable and enjoyable. Our aspiration is to act as an interpreter of our changing worlds between industry and the user. The embracing of technological advances will allow industrial design to become a truly expressive discipline." PEARSONLLOYD

1. **Easy** Sofa daybed Series for Walter
Knoll, 2002
2. ↓ **Flow** Lounge chair and ottoman for
Walter Knoll, 2001

3

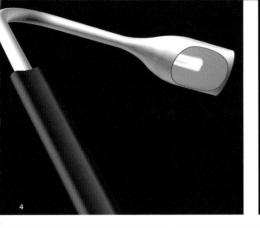

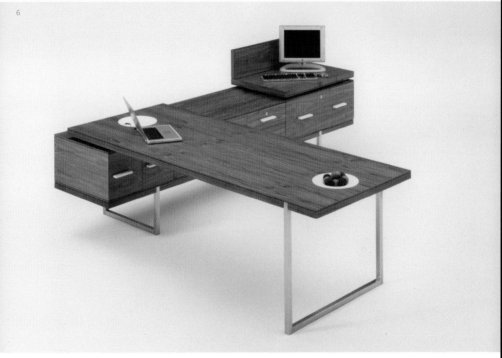

3. **Homer** personal mobile hot-desking unit for Knoll International, 1997-98

4. **Westminster Eye** street light and canopy light for Westminster City Council, 1999-2001

5. **Westminster Eye** street light for Westminster City Council, 1999-2001

6. Executive desking system. Power access through corian grommet in table surface for Samas Roneo, 2001.

"The best is yet to come."

Jorge Pensi

Jorge Pensi, Jorge Pensi Diseño, Pza. Berenguer 1, 08 002 Barcelona, Spain
T +34 93 310 3279 F: +34 93 315 1370 pensi@idgrup.ibernet.com

"A designer approaches an object in a similar way to an author – visually and conceptually weaving a story from an original mind's eye image. The most important difference, however, is that the designer usually works with a client, who specifies the theme and framework in which the creative process must take place. The client is the first input of the creative process, the person responsible for making the designer 'believe' in the inspiration before the first mental images (that make any sense) appear. In some projects the image is created in advance, while in others it is merely a rough, fuzzy concept that needs to be verified by several three-dimensional models and prototypes. In this sense, design is similar to architecture in that it relies on a process of trial and error.

The designer lives between two worlds – the subjective and the objective. The first world is based on symbols, originality and the relatively immutable and intrinsic nature of objects. It is connected to the magic of creativity, the influence of history and memory, and the great masters and visionaries of the design field. The second world is the real world, which is related to markets, investments, costs, the manufacturer and the production schedule. One world represents desire and the other, reality. The closer our desires are to reality, the better the design will be. The ability of an object to stir emotions comes from a process of development, where desires cannot be betrayed by reality and where the connection between the two worlds remains intact." JORGE PENSI

1. **Peppermint** armchair for Kron, 2000
2. ↓ **Chocolate** sofa for Perobell, 1999

3. ← **Duna** chair for Cassina, 1998
4. **Techne** office seating system for Kitto, 2000
5. **Nite** table & pendant lamp for B. Lux, 1998
6. **Hega** table & sideboard for Azcue, 2000
7. **Goya** wall-bookcase for Casprini, 1998

"Design must offer people an alternative way of living – it must answer the aspirations of people in terms of well-being and happiness."

Christophe Pillet

Christophe Pillet, 81 Rue Saint-Maur, 75011 Paris, France
T +33 1 48 06 78 31 F +33 1 48 06 78 32 cpillet@club-internet.fr

"If in the past design has concentrated mainly on producing solutions for specific problems of function, ergonomics, economy and aesthetics, it will tend in the future to liberate itself more and more from these specific concerns in order to become a discipline primarily devoted to the invention of environments for individuals.
Freeing itself from the systems that generated it, design will work on a more global scale on alternative and innovative lifestyles, on scenarios imagined that are driven by the desire for a better way of living."

CHRISTOPHE PILLET

1. **Sunset Lounge** armchair for Cappellini, 1998
2. ↓ **Ultra Living** sofa for E&Y, 1998

3

3. Saucepan for the **Pots and Pans** microwave experimental project for Whirlpool, 2000
4. **Video Lounge** chaise longue for Domeau & Perès, 1998
5. **C&C** table on castors for Fiam, 2000
6. **C&C** table for Fiam, 2000

"We jumble up typologies, mix references, manipulate codes, usages, techniques, forms and enjoy re-inventing our everyday habits."

RADI Designers

RADI Designers, 89, rue de Turenne, 75 003 Paris, France
T +33 1 42 71 29 57 F +33 1 42 71 29 62 info@radidesigners.com www.radidesigners.com

"Our work at RADI encompasses a broad range of projects, among them product design, stage sets, interior architecture and furniture design. In every one of our designs we endeavour to re-think the domestic, professional and public context and to breathe new life into the narrative of everyday life by re-inventing the most quotidian of objects and dreaming up new kinds of uses. As a group we have developed products that establish a close relationship between the imaginative and the functional realms. In these products we like to confound the rules, blur relations, manipulate techniques and combine typologies in wholly new ways. By subjecting received ideas to distortion, we invent new options for the interpretation of things in our environment and for contact with them. Deploying our philosophy of design in deliberately displaced modes, we are attempting to figure out a vision of the future in an unusual manner." RADI DESIGNERS

1. **Tempo Class** inflight tray for Air France,
2000
2. ↓ **Sleeping cat** carpet, limited edition,
Galerie Kreo Paris 1999.

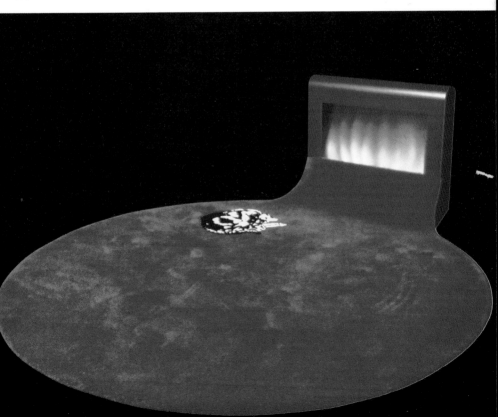

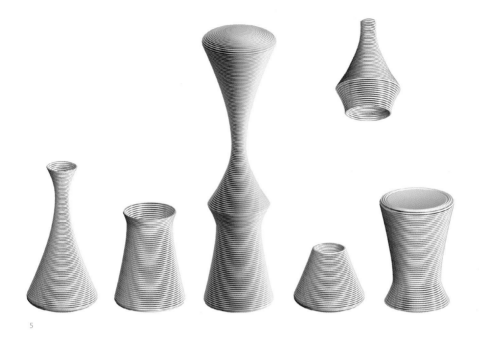

5

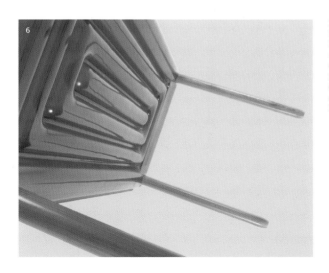

6

3.-4. ← **Fabulation** installation for the
Fondation Cartier pour l'art contemporain,
Paris, 1999
5. **Do Cut Together** from **Do Create**
collection, Robert Stadler/RADI
DESIGNERS, for Do-Foundation, 2001
6. **Twintable** from the Twin-sheet
collection, for Carte Blanche VIA, Paris
2000.

"My work is always a link between
simplicity, function and aesthetic values."

Ingegerd Råman

Ingegerd Råman, Bergsgatan 53, 11231 Stockholm, Sweden
T/F +46 8 650 2824 per.larsson@orrefors.se

"In the future, a designer's cultural and geographical background will
become increasingly significant. Heritage and tradition will be important stimuli in the creation and interpretation of concrete objects.
However, the qualities of a particular object will not be judged on the
basis of form and function alone. Designers will have to take an active
part in the entire industrial process and become stakeholders in their
works' production. Designers should participate in the development of
new techniques and materials, remaining alert to the environmental
impact and energy demands of production. They should be aware of
every aspect of the complicated process by which their pieces are
realised. The role of a designer will therefore be akin to that of a
researcher. For young artists, teamwork will be paramount in the
creation of independent, innovative design." INGEGERD RÅMAN

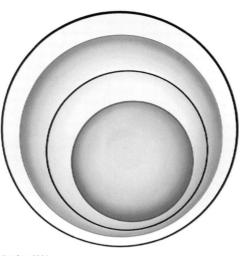

1.-2. **Babushka** bowls and jug for Orrefors, 2001

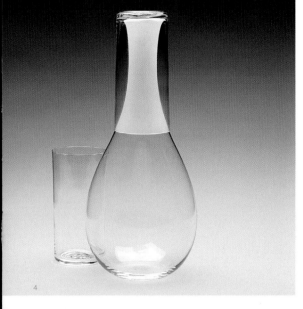

4

3. ← **Skyline** vases for Orrefors, 2000
4. **A Drop of Water** decanter and glass
for Orrefors, 2000
5. **Slowfox** vase for Orrefors, 2000

5

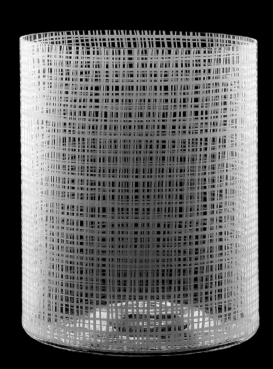

"Design is the whole experience of living."

Karim Rashid

Karim Rashid, 357, W 17th Street, New York, NY 10011, USA
T +1 212 929 8657 F +1 212 929 0247 office@karimrashid.com www.karimrashid.com

"Products must deal with our emotional ground and increase the popular imagination and experience. Diversity, variance, multiplicity and change are part of every whole construct. Industrial design is a creative act, a political act, a physical act and a socially interactive process that is greater than the physical form itself – its result is manifested in aesthetic forms, the content inspired by all the possibilities of our contemporary conditions.

In the controversial arguments about excess, sustainability and market seduction, I believe that every new object should replace three. Better products edit the marketplace. I believe objects should not be obstacles in life but raptures of experience. I try to develop objects as destressers – objects that bring enjoyment and simplify tasks while increasing our level of engagement and of beauty. Our lives are elevated when we experience beauty, comfort, luxury, performance and utility acting seamlessly together. Beauty is a deeper, inseparable relationship between the inner and the outer, an osmosis of aesthetics. Beauty is not a question of taste, or personal likes and dislikes but a learned appreciation, an experiential process. This underlying depth of beauty means that content plays a primary role in the beauty of things. Paintings, objects, art, architecture, space, all manifest their aesthetics through their content. The visual effect and the concept are one. Something beautiful has content." KARIM RASHID

1. **Pendant** lamp for George Kovacs Lighting, 1999
2. ↓ **Omni** reconfigurable seating object for Galerkin Furniture, 1999

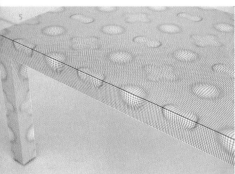

3. ← **OH** stacking chair for Umbra, 1999
4. **Sofa One** for Galerkin Furniture, 1999
5. **Morphscape** table (one-off), 2000
6. **Sumo** bowl, **Jambo** tray, **Rimbowl** and **Tribowl** bowls for Umbra, 1999
7. **Garbo** and **Garbino** wastepaper baskets for Umbra, 1996

"Low-tech choices for a digital era."

Timo Salli

Timo Salli, Muotoilutoimisto Salli Ltd., Meritullinkatu 11, 00 170 Helsinki, Finland
T +358 9 681 37700 F +358 9 278 2277 salli@timosalli.com

"I question how we look at things and whether this behaviour can be a motive to make functional objects. Could a fireplace replace a television? When stared at, both have a deeper purpose – they erase your memory until it is downloaded. Connecting the function of a mirror with that of a lamp is a way of producing a double meaning for one object. When the light is turned off it can be used as a mirror to reflect daylight, while during the evening it can be used both as a light-source and as a mirror, to see with and to be seen. Our homes are saturated with objects that we no longer notice. By reinterpreting the relics in the home, I aim for a more direct and meaningful contact between people and furniture." TIMO SALLI

1. **Jack in the Box** television set (self-production), 1997
2. ↓ **Zik Zak** collapsible chair (one-off for Snowcrash exhibition), 1997

3. ← **Tramp** easy chair (prototype) for Cappellini, 1997
4. **LampLamp** mirror lamp (self-production), 2000
5. **Power Ranger** chair (one-off), 1996
6. **TimoTimo** lamp (prototype), 1999

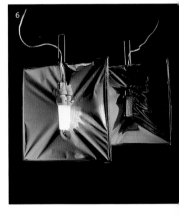

"We live in a society that accepts uncertainty as a principle and disregards the security that accompanies ideology."

SowdenDesign

Georg J. Sowden & Hiroshi Ono, SowdenDesign, Corso di Porta Nuova 46, 20 121 Milan, Italy
T +39 02 653 089   F +39 02 657 0228   milan@sowdendesign.com   www.sowdendesign.com

"The nature of the studio's work is determined by the fact that we do the design and the engineering at the same time – to divide them would be artificial. The way that things are assembled is so important, as it is in fashion and music. The engineering in products is like the precision of the cut in clothes or the sensitivity of the touch in music. Engineering is the execution that directs manufacturing industries. Manufacturing needs to be done carefully: modern aesthetics, like modern lifestyles, are very fragile. I do not mean this in a weak sense: I mean they are fast, they disregard monumentality, they thrive on diversity. I believe that it is quite unrealistic to try to put order into our environment but, if one thing can give sense to its fragility, the key is the quality of our manufacturing as we build an ever-changing collage of unrelated objects, which becomes the world in which we live."

GEORGE J. SOWDEN

1. **Toaster** for Guzzini, 2001
2. ↓ **Public Internet Terminal** for
American Airports (kiosk arrangement)
for Get2Net, 1999

3

4

3. **Rotor 2000** outdoor public telephone
for I. P. M., 1998
4. **Web payphone** for Nextera, 2000
5. **Rotor 2000** outdoor public web access
telephone for I. P. M., 1998
6. **Calculator** (study for Olivetti), 1999

5

6

"The 21st century will be immaterial and human."

Philippe Starck

Philippe Starck, Agence Philippe Starck, 18/20 rue du Faubourg de Temple, 75011 Paris, France
T +33 1 48 07 54 54 F +33 1 48 07 54 64 starck@starcknetwork.com
www.philippe-starck.com

"Today, the problem is not to produce more so that you can sell more. The fundamental question is that of the product's right to exist. And it is the designer's right and duty, in the first place, to question the legitimacy of the product, and that is how he too comes to exist. Depending on what answer he comes up with, one of the most positive things a designer can do is to refuse to do anything. This isn't always easy. He should refuse, nevertheless, when the object already exists and functions perfectly well. Simply to repeat it would be a venal act, and one which has serious consequences, impoverishing the wealth of the Earth, and impoverishing and dulling the minds of people ... We have to replace beauty, which is a cultural concept, with goodness, which is a humanist concept. The object must be of good quality, it must satisfy one of the key modern parameters, which is to be long-lived ... A good product is a product which lasts." PHILIPPE STARCK

1. **Low Cost Clock** for Seven Eleven, 1998
2. ↓ **Gaoua** duffle bag on wheels for Samsonite, 2000

3

4

5

6

7

3. **TeddyBearBand** toy (Catalogue GOOD
GOODS-La Redoute) for
Moulin Roty, 1998
4. **Motó 6,5** motorcycle for Aprilia, 1995
5. **Low Cost Watch** for Seven Eleven, 1998
6.-7. **Starck with Virgin theme CD**
(Catalogue GOOD GOODS-La Redoute)
for La Redoute, 1998

"I believe design is like poetry: absolute and precise with the minimal use of means employed to achieve the maximal result."

Ilkka Suppanen

Ilkka Suppanen, Studio Ilkka Suppanen, Punavuorenkatu 1A 7b, 00 120 Helsinki, Finland
T +358 9 622 78737 F +358 9 622 3093 info@suppanen.com www.suppanen.com

"I believe the situation of design today is similar to that of psychology in the 19th century – a practice with very little history or reputation. Psychology was not even regarded as a science then. It only became such as a result of the pioneering work of 'Mr' Freud. And as we know, the whole of the 20th century was the century of psychology. As a discipline, it became one of the most popular and quoted sciences only because of the perseverance and strong personality of Freud.
Like psychology in its early days, design is a practice that is not yet seen as scientifically important. It is quite unlike its 'big brother', architecture. I wish I could predict that design will have a future similar to that which psychology once had and that it too will become a respected science. Perhaps this will only happen if something like the strength and vision of Freud is widely embraced." ILKKA SUPPANEN

1. **Game-shelf** for Snowcrash, 1999
2. ↓ **Flying carpet** sofa for Cappellini, 1998

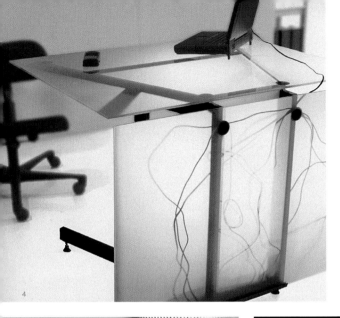

4

3. ← **Airbag** chair for Snowcrash,
1997 – co-designed with Pasi Kolhonen
4. **Luminet** office system for Luminet,
1996
5. Detail of **Airbag** chair for Snowcrash,
1997 – co-designed with Pasi Kolhonen
6. **Roll-light** floor lamp for Snowcrash,
1997

5

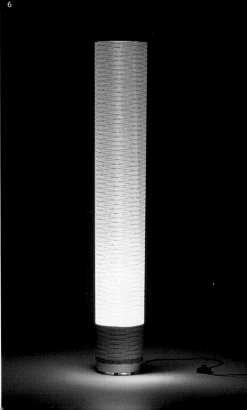

6

"I wonder if true inventions aren't always tied to an economy of the material and physical means used."

Martin Szekely

Martin Szekely, 111, Rue des Pyrénées, 75020 Paris, France
T +33 1 43 71 07 18   F +33 1 43 71 07 27   www.martinszekely.com

"Today, I see my work as detached from expressionism of the drawing. This idea grew out of my experience in industrial design which is directed at the broadest possible public. My aim is to achieve an economy in the result which can't even be defined as minimalist: a commonplace." MARTIN SZEKELY

1. **La Brique à Fleurs Vallauris** flowerpot for
Galerie Kreo, 1998
2. ↓ **Table 00 with bench** for Galerie Kreo,
2000

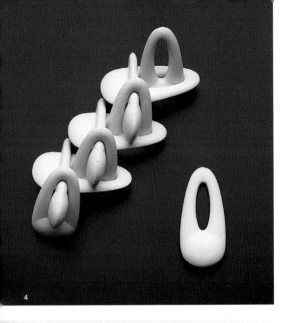

3. ← **Corolle** power pylons for Transel/EDF, 1994
4. **Reine de Saba** jewellery (chain and bracelet), resin model for Hermès, 1996
5. **L'Armoire** cabinet for Galerie Kreo, 1999
6. **Cork** chair for Galerie Kreo, 2000

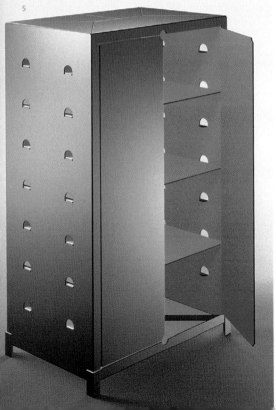

"The best products come from design
thinking that is interwoven with your
long-term business strategy."

Tangerine

Tangerine Product Direction and Design, 8, Baden Place, Crosby Row,
London SE1 1YW, England
T +44 20 7357 0966 F +33 20 7357 0784 martin@tangerine.net www.tangerine.net

"Really positive things are happening at the start of the 21st century in
the areas of brand and multi-media design. Companies have begun to
recognise that their brands are of tremendous value, expressing far
more than just the identity of a company; in many cases even typifying
the attitude and behaviour of the company. The surge of growth in the
multi-media sector will connect customers to companies in rich and
varied ways, enabling more diverse and extended forms of dialogue to
take place.
The hope I have for the future (and we have encountered many
examples of it recently) is that companies will wake up to the fact that
the customer cannot be fooled for too long. The best products do not
come from planning based on the benchmarking of competitors, or
from widgets spun out of R&D departments. The best products come
from observing people and learning about how they live, think, behave
etc. Designers can then bring business ethos, brand values and product
values together with core values from the life of the user, to define the
spirit and substance of new and better products." TANGERINE

1. **Jasperware** experimental design for Waterford Wedgwood, 1997
2. ↓ **Club World seat-bed** for British Airways, 2000

3. **Chaplet** e/web videophone for Chaplet
Information Systems, 1997

"My role as a designer is to provoke change."

Jean-Pierre Vitrac

Jean-Pierre Vitrac, Vitrac (Pool) Design Consultance, 98, Rue de l'Ouest, 75 014 Paris, France
T +33 1 40 44 09 50 F +33 1 40 44 7980 vitrac@design-pool.com www.design-pool.com

"Design has a future! Yes, but what kind? What is certain is that creativity is going to play an increasingly important role in our societies. The most obvious trend during the last few years has been an increasing break-up of the different genres or disciplines. Increasing diversity of expression as well as greater ease and freedom of communication allow both individuals and enterprises to attain a new kind of awareness: innovation as a normal component of any undertaking. It is not so important for the motivation to be an economic one. Nor is it so important to be moving towards an ever more complex context – which is what makes the design profession so interesting. The reality is that the necessities of evolution bring more reflection, more sense into our 'productions'. More and more people are beginning to feel concerned about design and are therefore entering into the creative process. Instead of continuing the process of simply consuming identical products, I think that there will be a movement towards greater selectivity which will result in greater diversity and better quality in the future. And so as far as design is concerned, everything is open."

JEAN-PIERRE VITRAC

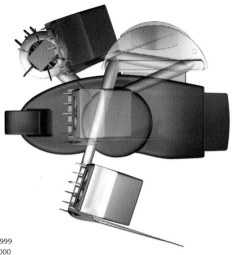

1. **Carisma** dental unit for Fedesa, 1999
2. ↓ **Urban furniture** for Giraudy, 2000

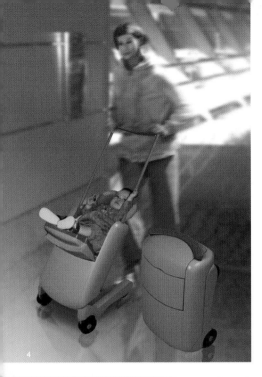

3. ← **Information meeting point** for Arcomat Mobilier Urbain, 1999
4. **Baby Move** child traveller for Marco Skates, 1999
5. **U.Bik** exterior lighting for Noral, 1999
6. **Flash Vote** everday democracy for Expo 2000
7. **Crossing Radio** for Arco Impex, 2001

4

5

6

7

"We are here to create an environment of love, live with passion and make our most exciting dreams come true."

Marcel Wanders

Marcel Wanders, Jacob Catskade 35, 1052 BT Amsterdam, The Netherlands
T +31 20 422 1339 F +31 20 422 7519 marcel@marcelwanders.nl www.marcelwanders.com

"Our culture lacks respect for the old. We prefer the new to the old. New things are considered better, old news is no news. Products have to be smooth, taut and flawless. Sadly, it appears that this fixation on the new and the young is even stronger among designers than other people. I suspect that they (including myself) have even less respect than others for the old, as it is their profession to create new things. We suffer from what I call 'baby-face fixation'.
The life expectancy of baby-face designs is very short. This makes them temporary friends on which users cannot truly rely and which will never become a real part of their lives. Baby-face fixation is a problem in a world in which lasting quality and a unique bond between product and user is important.
Since I would like many of my products to enter into a long-term relationship with the user, I use both old and new metaphors in the materials and material expressions that I apply. By using old metaphors in my products, I communicate a respect for old age in general. This leads to a more respectful, more acceptable and more natural ageing of my products (age with dignity). These products have the possibility of gaining quality during their life, they are more durable and it is possible to have a long-lasting relationship with them.
Durability in the field of ideas, relationships, objects, and so on, not only to create a world that is less wasteful but also to create deeper and more meaningful relationships with our environment." MARCEL WANDERS

1. **VIP** chair for Moooi, 2000
2. ↓ **Textile wall for a Lunch
Lounge** for Co van der Horst, 1999

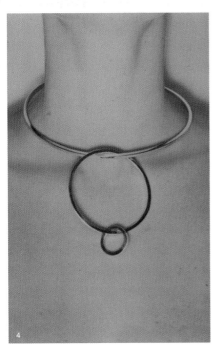

3. ← **Shadows Series** table and floor
lamps for Cappellini, 1998
4. **Trinity** necklace for Chi ha paura, 1998
5. **Henna** table for Cappellini, 2000
6. **Nomad** carpet for Cappellini, 1999

"I'm just looking at new yet rational ways of realizing objects."

Michael Young

Michael Young, MY Studio, PO Box 498, 121 Reykjavik, Iceland
T +354 561 2327 F +354 561 2315 michaelyoung@simnet.is www.michael-young.com

"Currently, 'designed' objects challenge only a tiny percentage of the world market. The majority of products are in real terms engineered copies. Present-day technology means that a designed product may be copied by mass-market competitors in less than one year. Protecting an innovation in either manufacturing technique or idea would seem to be of utmost importance to design in the future. Especially so when computer programmes will soon be able to morph surprisingly beautiful objects at random without designers and provide all the necessary production data as well. On a positive note, this would leave design in a position where innovation will become the human aspect rather than style." MICHAEL YOUNG

1. **MY 083** table for Magis, 2001
2. ↓ **Armed chair** for Cappellini, 1999

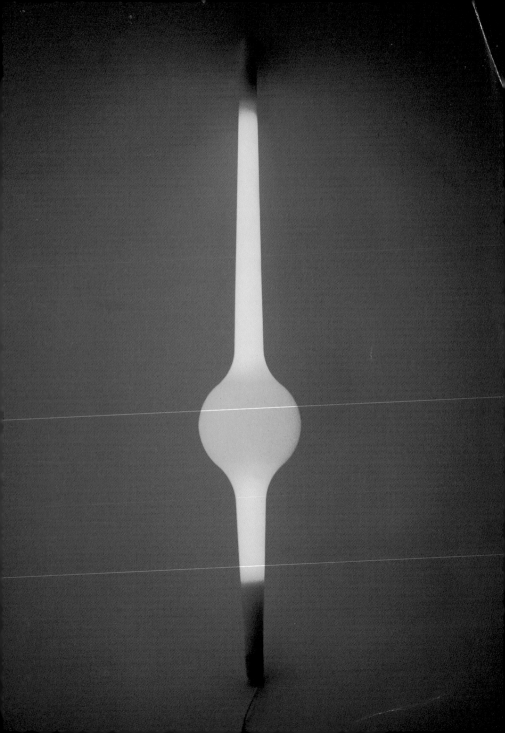

4

5

6

3. ← **Sticklight** for Eurolounge, 1999
4.-7. **Astro Bar** nightclub (interiors),
Reykjavik, 2000

We are immensely grateful to those designers, design groups, photographers and manufacturers who have allowed us to reproduce images from their archives. The publisher has endeavoured to respect the rights of third parties and if any rights have been overlooked in individual cases, the mistake will be correspondingly amended where possible.

L = left
R = right
T = top
C = centre
B = bottom

3 Azumi, photo: Kumi Saito
9 Ford Motor Company
10 Studio Aisslinger, photo: Steffen Jänicke
11 T Studio Aisslinger
11 B Studio Aisslinger, photo: Steffen Jänicke
12 T L & T R Zanotta, photos: Adriano Brusaferri
12 B Studio Aisslinger, photo: Philip Radowitz
13 T R Studio Aisslinger
13 C & B Studio Aisslinger, photos: Steffen Jänicke
14 Ron Arad Associates, photo: Perry Hagopian
15 T Ron Arad Associates, photo: Guido Pedron
15 B Ron Arad Associates, photo: Wilhelm Moser
16 Ron Arad Associates, photo: Wilhelm Moser
17 Moroso, photos: A. Paderni
18-19 Jane Atfield
20 Fiell International Ltd., photo: Paul Chave
21 Jane Atfield

21 B R Oreka Kids
22 Azumi, photo: Julian Hawkins
23 T Azumi, photo: Michael Tesmann
23 B Azumi, photo: Julian Hawkins
24 T L Azumi, photo: Hiroyuki Hirai
24 T R Azumi, photo: Thomas Dobbie
24 B L Azumi, photo: Shin Azumi
24 B R Azumi
25 T Azumi, photo: Thomas Dobbie
25 B L Azumi, photo: Julian Hawkins
25 B R Azumi
26 Sebastian Bergne
27 T Sebastian Bergne, photo: WMF
27-28 Sebastian Bergne, photos: Authentics, Artipresent GmbH
29 T Sebastian Bergne, photo: Vitra – Hans Hansen
29 B Sebastian Bergne, photo: Wireworks UK
30-33 Ronan & Erwan Bouroullec, photos: M. Legall
34-37 Studio Brown
38 Studio Campana, photo: J. R. Duran
39-41 Studio Campana, photos: Andrés Otero
42 Antonio Citterio, photo: Gitty Darugar
43 T Antonio Citterio, photo: Hackman
43 B Antonio Citterio, photo: B&B Italia – Fabrizio Bergamo
44 Antonio Citterio, photos: B&B Italia
45 L Antonio Citterio, photo: Flos
45 R Antonio Citterio, photo: Hackman
46-49 Dahlström Design
50-53 Emmanuel Dietrich
54-57 Elephant Design
58 Naoto Fukasawa, photo: IDEO-Japan
59-61 IDEO-Japan
62 photo: © Mario Pignata Monti
63 T photo: © Mario Pignata Monti
63 B Jean Marc Gady, photo: Jeoffrey Bello
64 Jean Marc Gady, photo: © Vincent Muracciole

65 photos: © Mario Pignata Monti
66 Giovannoni Design
67 T Giovannoni Design, photo: Alessi
67 B Giovannoni Design, photo: Segno
68 Giovannoni Design, photo: Alessi
69 Giovannoni Design, photo: Magis
70 Konstantin Grcic, photo: © Daniel Mayer
71 T Konstantin Grcic
71 B Konstantin Grcic, photo: © Eva Jünger
72 Konstantin Grcic, photo: ClassiCon
73 T & C Konstantin Grcic
73 B Konstantin Grcic, photo: littala
78 Matthew Hilton, photo: Corinna Dean
79 T SCP Ltd.
79 B Oreka Kids
80 Authentics GmbH
81 T & C L Driade
81 C R & B SCP Ltd.
82-84 Inflate, photos: Jason Tozer
85 Inflate, photo: Jason Tozer
85 T L Inflate, photo: Jason Tozer
85 T R & B Inflate
86-87 James Irvine
88-89 Arabia
90 Apple Computer, photo: Catherine Ledman
91-93 Apple Computer
94 Jam, photos: Jason Tozer
95 Jam, photo: Paul Musso
96 Jam
97 Jam, photos: Jason Tozer
98 littala
99 T Hackman
99 B littala, photo: Marco Melander
100 T Arabia
100 B L & B R littala
101 littala
102-103 Ross Lovegrove/Studio X, photos: John Ross
104 T Ross Lovegrove, photo: John Ross
104 B Japan Airlines, photo: Lee Funnell for *Domus* magazine

105 Ross Lovegrove/Studio X, photo: John Ross
106-109 Lunar Design
110 Enzo Mari
111 T Zani e Zani, photo: Marirosa Ballo
111 B Magis Srl
112 Glaskoch Leonardo
113 T Arte e Cuoio
113 B L Zani e Zani, photo: Marirosa Ballo
113 B R Arte e Cuoio
114-117 Ford Motor Company
118 Alberto Meda
119 T Alberto Meda, photo: Alias
119 B Alberto Meda, photo: Luceplan
120 Alberto Meda, photo: Vitra
121 Alberto Meda
122 Office for Design, photo: Emily Anderson
123-125 Office for Design
126 Marc Newson, photo: Karin Catt
127-129 Marc Newson
130 PearsonLloyd, photo: Sandra Lousada
131-133 PearsonLloyd
134 Jorge Pensi
135 T Jorge Pensi
135 B IDPA, Perobell
136 Jorge Pensi, photos: IDPA
137 Jorge Pensi, photos: IDPA
138 Christophe Pillet
139 T Christophe Pillet, photo: Cappellini
139 B Christophe Pillet, photo: E&Y
140 Christophe Pillet
141 T Christophe Pillet, photo: Domeau & Pérès
141 C & B Christophe Pillet, photos: Fiam
142-145 Radi Designers
143 B S. Garcia
145 B Joffrey Bello
146 Orrefors, photo: Hans Gedda
147 Orrefors, photos: Rolf Lind
148 Orrefors, photos: Roland Persson
149 T Orrefors, photo: Bengt Wanselius
149 B Orrefors, photo: Rolf Lind

150-151 Karim Rashid
152 Karim Rashid, photo: Ilan Rubin
153 Karim Rashid
154 Muotoilutoimisto Salli Ltd., photo: Marja Helander
155 Muotoilutoimisto Salli Ltd., photos: Marco Melander
156 Muotoilutoimisto Salli Ltd., photo: Ulla Hassinen
157 T Muotoilutoimisto Salli Ltd., photo: Timo Salli
157 B L & B R Muotoilutoimisto Salli Ltd., photos: Marco Melander
158-159 Sowden Design Associates
160 T L & T R Sowden Design Associates
160-161 B Sowden Design Associates, photo: Studio Gallo
161 T Sowden Design Associates, photo: Ilvio Gallo
162 Philippe Stark
163 T Philippe Starck, photo: Studio Bleu – Michel Lelièvre
163 B Samsonite
164 Philippe Starck, photo: Studio Bleu – Michel Lelièvre for GOOD GOODS/La Redoute
165 T Philippe Starck, photo: Studio Bleu – Michel Lelièvre for GOOD GOODS/La Redoute
165 B L Philippe Starck, photo: Studio Bleu – Michel Lelièvre
165 B R Philippe Starck, photo: Studio Bleu – Michel Lelièvre for GOOD GOODS/ La Redoute
166 Ilkka Suppanen
167 T Snowcrash
167 B Cappellini
168 Snowcrash
169 T Luminet
169 B L & B R Snowcrash
170 Martin Szekely, photo: P. Capellamm
171 T Martin Szekely, photo: S. Demailly
171 B Martin Szekely, photo: Galerie Kreo

172 Martin Szekely, photo: Alain Dovifat
173 T Martin Szekely, photo: Hermès
173 B L Galerie Kreo
173 B R Galerie Kreo, photo: M. Domage
174 Tangerine, photo: Dario Rumbo
175 T Tangerine
175 B Tangerine, photo: British Airways
176-177 Tangerine, photos: Moggy
178-181 Vitrac Design-Pool
182 Wanders Wonders, photo: HK Kamerbeek
183 T Wanders Wonders, photo: Maarten van Houten
184-185 B Wanders Wonders
186-189 MY Studio

Graphic Design for the 21st Century
Charlotte & Peter Fiell /
Flexi-cover, 640 pp. / € 29.99 /
$ 39.99 / £ 19.99 / ¥ 5.900

Scandinavian Design
Charlotte & Peter Fiell /
Flexi-cover, 704 pp. / € 29.99 /
$ 39.99 / £ 19.99 / ¥ 5.900

Designing the 21st Century
Ed. Charlotte & Peter Fiell /
Flexi-cover, 576 pp. / € 29.99 /
$ 39.99 / £ 19.99 / ¥ 5.900

"These books are beautiful objects, well-designed and lucid." —*Le Monde*, Paris, on the ICONS series

"Buy them all and add some pleasure to your life."

Alchemy & Mysticism
Alexander Roob

All-American Ads 40⁵
Ed. Jim Heimann

All-American Ads 50⁵
Ed. Jim Heimann

All-American Ads 60⁵
Ed. Jim Heimann

Angels
Gilles Néret

Architecture Now!
Ed. Philip Jodidio

Art Now
Eds. Burkhard Riemschneider,
Uta Grosenick

Berlin Style
Ed. Angelika Taschen

Chairs
Charlotte & Peter Fiell

Design of the 20ᵗʰ Century
Charlotte & Peter Fiell

Design for the 21ˢᵗ Century
Charlotte & Peter Fiell

Devils
Gilles Néret

Digital Beauties
Ed. Julius Wiedemann

Robert Doisneau
Ed. Jean-Claude Gautrand

East German Design
Ralf Ulrich / Photos: Ernst
Hedler

Egypt Style
Ed. Angelika Taschen

M.C. Escher

Fashion
Ed. The Kyoto Costume
Institute

HR Giger
HR Giger

Grand Tour
Harry Seidler,
Ed. Peter Gössel

Graphic Design
Ed. Charlotte & Peter Fiell

Havana Style
Ed. Angelika Taschen

Homo Art
Gilles Néret

Hot Rods
Ed. Coco Shinomiya

Hula
Ed. Jim Heimann

India Bazaar
Samantha Harrison,
Bari Kumar

Industrial Design
Charlotte & Peter Fiell

Japanese Beauties
Ed. Alex Gross

Kitchen Kitsch
Ed. Jim Heimann

Krazy Kids' Food
Eds. Steve Roden,
Dan Goodsell

Las Vegas
Ed. Jim Heimann

Mexicana
Ed. Jim Heimann

Mexico Style
Ed. Angelika Taschen

Morocco Style
Ed. Angelika Taschen

**Extra/Ordinary Objects,
Vol. I**
Ed. Colors Magazine

**Extra/Ordinary Objects,
Vol. II**
Ed. Colors Magazine

Paris Style
Ed. Angelika Taschen

Penguin
Frans Lanting

20ᵗʰ Century Photography
Museum Ludwig Cologne

Pin-Ups
Ed. Burkhard Riemschneider

Provence Style
Ed. Angelika Taschen

Pussycats
Gilles Néret

Safari Style
Ed. Angelika Taschen

Seaside Style
Ed. Angelika Taschen

Albertus Seba. Butterflies
Irmgard Müsch

**Albertus Seba. Shells &
Corals**
Irmgard Müsch

Starck
Ed Mae Cooper, Pierre Doze,
Elisabeth Laville

Surfing
Ed. Jim Heimann

Sydney Style
Ed. Angelika Taschen

Tattoos
Ed. Henk Schiffmacher

Tiffany
Jacob Baal-Teshuva

Tiki Style
Sven Kirsten

Tuscany Style
Ed. Angelika Taschen

Women Artists
in the 20ᵗʰ and 21ˢᵗ Century
Ed. Uta Grosenick